BUSINESS DATA PROCESSING: AN INTRODUCTION

Gershon J. Wheeler and Donlan F. Jones
Sylvania Electric Products, Inc.

ADDISON-WESLEY PUBLISHING COMPANY, INC.
Reading, Massachusetts, U.S.A.
ADDISON-WESLEY (CANADA) LIMITED
Don Mills, Ontario

ADDISON–WESLEY PUBLISHING COMPANY, INC.
READING, MASSACHUSETTS · Palo Alto · London
NEW YORK · DALLAS · ATLANTA · BARRINGTON, ILLINOIS

ADDISON–WESLEY (CANADA) LIMITED
DON MILLS, ONTARIO

Preface

This book may be used as a text in a first semester course in business data processing. The emphasis is on *business,* and to this end the techniques described in each chapter are related to business operations and procedures. However, no prior knowledge either of business methods or of data processing is required.

The Instructors' Manual indicates what should be covered in each lesson and has answers to the questions at the end of each chapter. We have also included additional questions for each chapter as suggested examination problems.

We would like to acknowledge the assistance of the following for their helpful criticism and suggestions during the preparation of the manuscript: Mr. Leland Baldwin, Chief, Bureau of Junior College Technical/ Vocational Education; Professor Philip Nash, Director of Data Processing, Monterey Peninsula College; Mr. John C. Newell, Instructor, Department of Data Processing, Chabot College.

Mountain View, California   G. J. W.
March 1966   D. F. J.

Contents

PART 1   What is Data Processing?

Chapter 1   Introduction

1–1	Data processing: Introduction	3
1–2	Types of computers	5
1–3	Uses of electronic data processing	5
1–4	Economic implications	6
1–5	Example	7

Student's Preface   11

Chapter 2   Data in Business

2–1	Business data	13
2–2	Creation of new data	13
2–3	Example	15
2–4	Manipulation of data	19

Chapter 3   History of Data Processing

3–1	Early calculators	22
3–2	Development of the modern computer	24

Chapter 4   Manual and Machine Data Processing

4–1	Manual data processing	28
4–2	Recording of manual data	30
4–3	Machine data processing	32
4–4	Programs	34

PART 2   Punched Card Data Processing

Chapter 5   Punched Cards

5–1	Introduction	41
5–2	Description of punched cards	42
5–3	Disadvantages of punched card processing	46

Chapter 6 Machines for Processing Cards

6–1 Introduction 48
6–2 Keypunch 49
6–3 Example 50
6–4 Verifier 54
6–5 Sorter 55
6–6 Interpreter 56
6–7 Collator 57
6–8 Reproducing punch 58
6–9 Accounting machine 59
6–10 Control circuits 60
6–11 Multipurpose machines 61
6–12 Electronic calculating punch 62

Chapter 7 Punched Cards in Business

7–1 Application of punched cards in business 64

PART 3 Computer Data Processing

Chapter 8 Parts of a Computer

8–1 Computer components 75
8–2 Storage 77
8–3 Arithmetic-logic 80
8–4 Control 82
8–5 Input 83
8–6 Output 85
8–7 The computer system 86

Chapter 9 Codes

9–1 Decimal and binary systems 90
9–2 Types of codes 93
9–3 Error deduction 96
9–4 Computer language 98

Chapter 10   Programming

    10–1   Programming instructions   100
    10–2   Computer languages   101
    10–3   Preparing a program   103
    10–4   Flow chart   104

Chapter 11   Writing the Program

    11–1   COBOL   111
    11–2   The COBOL program   113
    11–3   Program divisions   117
    11–4   COBOL form   117
    11–5   Writing a COBOL program   118

Chapter 12   Choosing a Computer

    12–1   Reasons for installing a computer   132
    12–2   What kind of computer?   133
    12–3   Erroneous fear of the computer   134
    12–4   Real time and batch processing   135
    12–5   Time sharing   135
    12–6   The future of the computer   136

    Answers to Odd-Numbered Questions   138

    Index   149

PART 1

What Is Data Processing?

1

Introduction

1-1 DATA PROCESSING: INTRODUCTION

The first electronic computer for business use was installed in 1954 at General Electric's Appliance Park. This was a Univac I Computer, specifically designed to handle routine bookkeeping tasks automatically and rapidly. At the time, it was generally believed that a few such computers, strategically located, could satisfy all the business computation needs in the country. Yet only ten years later, in 1964, more than 15,000 electronic business computers, worth about four billion dollars, were in use. The market is still growing and each year more computers are used for *business data processing.*

Before we can explain why the experts were so wrong in their estimates of the future of computers for data processing, we must know what the term *data processing* means. In the first place, data processing is nothing new. Whenever information is gathered or disseminated, we can say it is handled or processed. When the supermarket manager keeps track of his stock so that he knows when and what to reorder, his records are *data* and he is *processing* them. Likewise, when he calculates an employee's weekly paycheck on the basis of the number of hours worked, he is processing data. Of course, he does not call it that; possibly he refers to the first task as taking inventory and the second as bookkeeping. Data processing, then, is a term which encompasses any collection of facts, manipulation of information to get other facts, or output of information. It is possible that one of the first *data handlers* was Moses when he received the Ten Commandments from God and chiseled them on stone so that the people could read them.

The fact that electronic computers are now used for data processing has led the general public to believe that it is a mysterious, complicated science and that the computers are giant brains. Both notions are false. Basically, a computer is a high-speed adding machine which does what it is told to do. If the input data are varied even slightly, the computer cannot operate until it is programmed to accept the variations. The business operations it performs are impressive only because of the extremely high speed of manipulation, but most of these operations have been in use for decades. Unlike man, the computer performs repetitive calculations without getting tired or bored.

Before the advent of machines, data processing was done by hand. The bookkeeper in a concern kept records of purchases, sales, payrolls, taxes, and many other things. He was not given a fancy name, and if you had called the bookkeeper a data processor, he would probably have been insulted. As new machines were developed, some of the *manual* data processing jobs were taken over by *machine* data processing. For example, when new cash registers automatically registered the total of all sales that were rung up, it was no longer necessary for the bookkeeper to enter every sale and total all sales at the end of each day. The cash register performed one data-processing function, keeping a running total of the day's receipts.

Another routine task, addressing envelopes, was taken over by a machine called an *addressograph*. The newer addressographs are run by electricity and have moving parts and thus belong to the class of *electromechanical* devices. When data processing is done by a machine, whether operated manually or by electricity, we refer to it as *machine data processing*.

Although data processing is as old as history, the term itself was coined after the advent of the electronic computer. (Incidentally, the term must be an error coined by someone who did not realize that the word *data* is plural. Just as we speak of shoe manufacturing rather than *shoes* manufacturing, we should call our subject *datum* processing.) There is no doubt that data processing is now an important *discipline*, that is, a separate subject to study. The computer raised it from a hodgepodge of assorted bookkeeping tasks to its present status. When the Univac I was installed, routine bookkeeping chores that formerly took weeks were performed in hours or even minutes. As was mentioned before, the experts felt that a few such machines could solve all bookkeeping problems. What they failed to foresee was that once these ultrafast machines were installed, thinking people would use them to solve many problems that heretofore had remained unsolved because solutions would have required months of effort. This is a continuing process, and new uses for electronic computers are found almost daily. We will discuss some of these new uses in a later chapter.

1–2   TYPES OF COMPUTERS

It is necessary to distinguish between the desk-type calculators, sometimes called *electric* computers, and the *electronic* computers, which operate in thousandths, millionths, or even billionths of a second. The desk calculators are, of course, electromechanical devices, whereas the electronic computer is the heart of *electronic data processing* or EDP. There is a wide variety of electromechanical business machines: one special class of machine is the kind that operates using punched cards. *Business data processing* or BDP may be electronic data processing, punched-card data processing, machine data processing, manual data processing, or a combination of two or more of these. In general, if an electronic computer is used, we refer to the system as EDP, even if other machines are used in part of the system.

1–3   USES OF ELECTRONIC DATA PROCESSING

The first electronic business computers simply performed the usual data processing that business had been doing mechanically or manually. The computer's existence was justified because the work was performed faster, cheaper, and more accurately. However, the almost unbelievable speed of operation permitted the computer to be used for solving problems which required large quantities of computations. A trivial example of such a problem follows. A small boy is sent to the fruit store with two dollars and told to buy oranges, apples, and grapefruit. He must buy as many pieces of fruit as possible but, since his mother is afraid he might strain himself carrying the fruit home, she tells him he must not buy more than ten pounds of fruit. Now suppose an apple costs 5 cents and weighs ½ pound, an orange costs 8 cents and weighs 6 ounces, and a grapefruit costs 25 cents and weighs 1 pound. Obviously, for two dollars, the boy could buy 40 apples, but they would weigh 20 pounds, and his limit is 10 pounds. Or he could buy 8 grapefruit but they would weigh only 8 pounds. If the problem were given to a computer, it would run through every possible combination of fruits and would present the answer in a matter of seconds. In practical problems, there are many more variables to be compared in this type of *decision-making* problem. The mathematical name for this method is called *linear programming*, and it may involve hundreds of thousands of repetitive calculations. (The process is sometimes called *iteration*.) The computer has changed decision-making at the management level from an art to a science.

Another new use for computers, unforeseen by the experts in the early 1950's, is called *critical path analysis*. Again, a fancy name is used to describe an old problem, but the computer allows the manager to solve this problem scientifically, instead of by the seat of his pants. This is also easily described by a trivial example. A housewife wishes to prepare a dinner. She knows how long it takes to prepare the meat, potatoes, vegetables, and pie, and also that some items, such as pie, must be allowed to cool for a specified time. With little effort she can figure out when to start each item so that they will all be ready at the appointed time. In a business problem, there are far more items to complete, and the computer can analyze the problem and determine when each individual operation must begin and how long the total operation will take.

The biggest impact of the computer on business is in the concept of the *total system*. The word "system" could be "thing" and should cause no confusion. We speak of systems in the body: for example, the nervous system, the digestive system, etc. Each one of these is a subsystem of the larger thing we call the human system. In a similar manner, the computer and its accompanying paraphernalia form a data-processing *system*, which, in general, is part of the business. However, the concept of total system means simply that *all* collecting, processing, analyzing, and disseminating of information is continuous and immediate; all transactions are recorded as they happen. Everything that has happened, that is, all records, are contained in *memory*. Facilities for entering data or recording data are connected to the places where things happen. The airlines' reservation systems now operate in this fashion. The agent applies for a space while the customer waits. If a space is available, he writes the ticket, and the computer memory accepts this information as the ticket is being written.

1–4   ECONOMIC IMPLICATIONS

Since the computer does various tasks rapidly and automatically, many people fear it will eliminate their jobs. This is only superficially true for two reasons. In the first place the computer does jobs which would not otherwise be done because of lack of manpower. A good example of this antedates the electronic computer. In 1915, the Bell Telephone Company estimated that if the population grew as expected, the telephone call traffic would reach such a high volume that every eligible female in the country would be needed to man the switchboards. The dial telephone, an electric data-processing device, was developed to permit more calls to be handled faster, despite the lack of manpower.

In the second place, even if the computer eliminates some jobs, such as those of bookkeepers, it usually provides more jobs than it eliminates. This happens because the computer can be used to solve more problems, providing useful information for many different echelons in a business. The demand for personnel, experienced in EDP, is steadily increasing and will continue to do so for many years.

It is not too farfetched to believe that in the near future, even small businesses will find it economical to avail themselves of EDP. It is now possible for several businesses to share one central computer to which they are tied by telephone lines. Eventually data processing may be wired in like any other utility such as telephone, electricity or gas.

The business community today is getting to be a world of computers. The executive or manager who has no knowledge of electronic data processing is at a severe disadvantage. He does not have to be an expert or specialist, since he can hire experts, but he must be able to evaluate the performance of the people he hires and the new systems which are proposed. As computer capabilities are increased, the manager must update his knowledge to include the latest technology.

At nearly every echelon in a large business, a knowledge of business data processing is advantageous and often necessary. For instance, if a delivery truck must stop in 18 cities, the dispatcher can ask the computer in what order these cities should be visited to minimize mileage and get the answer in seconds. If past history is stored in a computer, it can detect trends from comparatively few new data, as was demonstrated in past presidential elections. This type of information is useful to buyers, salesmen, designers, and even public relations and advertising men.

1–5 EXAMPLE

Consider the case of a typical company with and without EDP. The XYZ Company in California, which has 500 employees, manufactures corduroy jackets for children. The jackets are in three colors, red, brown, and navy, and come in five sizes, or a total of 15 different combinations of size and color. Each jacket has four metal buttons.

In a typical day, orders arrive by mail directly from customers or are brought or phoned in by the XYZ salesmen. The customers are retail stores in seven Western states.

The orders are given to a foreman who determines how many of each of the 15 different types are to be manufactured. The patterns from which the cutters work include parts for four jackets in each size. (It is more economical to stack long layers of cloth and cut parts for four jackets at once than to pile up smaller layers, each of which contains enough material for only one jacket.) From his list of the quantity of each size and color, the foreman makes a chart for each size indicating how many layers of material of each color shall be used. The cutter piles up the layers of cloth and cuts through all simultaneously. It should be noted that if the quantity of a particular jacket type is not divisible by four, some extra jackets will be manufactured.

After the cloth is cut, the parts are dumped into baskets which are carried to the sewing machine operators, each of whom performs a repetitive operation. For example, one may sew on pockets, another may make buttonholes, etc. The finished jackets are inspected. They are then sorted by orders and wrapped for shipment. All packages go on the company's truck, for delivery either to the post office or to local customers. The *extra* jackets are placed in a sales room, where they may be shown as samples to prospective customers. Ideally, the foreman should check them each morning against his orders before making his cutting charts. In practice, it takes too much time to run through the racks. The extra jackets then accumulate until a buyer from a discount store appears and offers to buy all at cost.

The firm employs a buyer who must make sure that there is sufficient material and buttons on hand to meet orders. He is also responsible for pins, needles, thread, thimbles, and other items used in the trade. The receiving and shipping department must keep an inventory of packaging materials, and a maintenance man must keep the machines operating efficiently.

The bookkeeping department has the usual functions. The bookkeepers calculate the weekly gross pay for each employee by multiplying the hours worked in the week by the hourly rate. From this figure they must deduct taxes, social security, any pension or bond deductions, and thus calculate each paycheck. The checks must be typed and signed. (In a large organization, a signature stamp may be used.)

The incoming bills for materials and services must be checked, and checks mailed to vendors. Customers must be billed for orders. Receipts (incoming checks) must be recorded to the customers' credit, allowing discounts if necessary, and the checks must be deposited.

Records of all transactions must be kept carefully, and totals must be tabulated at periodic intervals for tax purposes. The employee must be furnished a statement showing his annual earnings and deductions for tax and social security. The government requires quarterly statements from the employer for the total of all the tax deductions and all the social security deductions.

In the absence of EDP, girls calculate the paychecks using electric desk calculators. It may take 10 girls a week to calculate the paychecks and type them. This is their only job, and the checks thus are paid a week late.

Invoices are typed and mailed by other girls, who may also take care of normal correspondence. Everyone is busy, orders keep coming in, and the company is making money, but it is not growing.

Now suppose a computer is installed just for bookkeeping. After the computer is programmed with information about each employee, it can take over the check-writing function. One girl is needed to punch the information about hours worked onto a card for each employee. The computer receives the information, calculates taxes, and other deductions, and prints out the paychecks. Further, it keeps a running record of total deductions of each type for each employee and totals of these totals for the company records. The payroll function may take less than one hour instead of one week.

The computer will also type invoices. Each sale and shipment is entered into the computer's memory as it occurs. The computer sorts these out, and when called, the invoices are typed out, summing up each customer's purchases for the whole month.

Since the bookkeeping functions take so little time, the manager of the XYZ Company decides to use the computer in other operations. Each incoming order is entered on the computer as it comes in. At any time, the computer can furnish the number of each of 15 jacket types on order. Further, once a suitable program has been entered, the computer can furnish the cutting charts at the push of a button. It can also furnish a list of extra jackets that have been made to date and can indicate how many are applicable to current orders. All this takes the foreman a few seconds instead of the hour or two normally required.

Several bookkeepers have been eliminated but a few programmers are needed. The manager also has added a data-processing expert on his staff. Using the computer to analyze the operations, it is possible to increase production so that the backlog of orders is reduced. This means increased capability. Since a few orders have been coming in by mail from states not covered by the XYZ salesmen, the manager decides to hire additional salesmen to cover four more states. The increased business which results means more jobs for cutters and sewing machine operators, but little increase in overhead since the computer handles the additional paper work.

BIBLIOGRAPHY

DAVIS, HARRY M., "Mathmatical Machines," *Scientific American*, April, 1949, pp. 29–39. This is a good general article which covers the field well. It is suitable as an introduction to the new machines which solve large scale mathematical problems.

NATIONAL CASH REGISTER CO., *History of Accounting*, 1964. This pamphlet lists the key events from the earliest recorded time to the present.

NATIONAL CASH REGISTER Co., *What is Data Processing? Electronic Data Processing Written for the Layman,* Book 1, SP-1553-A-D16QQQ. This pamphlet is an easy-to-read discussion of what data processing is and what it means in business.

These are all easy reading and well worth the additional effort.

QUESTIONS

1–1
What is meant by the term *data processing?*

1–2
List at least six methods or means of data processing other than those using punched-card data processing equipment or an electronic computer.

1–3
What are some reasons why a business would use an electronic computer or other business data processing equipment?

1–4
Because of the versatility and speed of computers, today's managers do not have to know anything about computers. *True* or *false?*

1–5
Discuss the statement, "When computers were first installed in this country people were quick to see that there would be a tremendous demand for computers because of the wide variety of possible applications."

1–6
Discuss the statement, "The use of computers and other data processing equipment will lead to widespread unemployment."

1–7
Distinguish between electronic data processing (EDP) and punched-card data processing.

1–8
What can be eliminated from business data-processing systems to increase the accuracy of those systems?

1–9
Computers are so expensive that small businesses are not able to afford using them. *True* or *false?*

1–10
Discuss the statement, "Since punched-card data processing equipment and computers operate at such fast speeds, there is not much demand for personnel trained in operating and programming the machines."

Student's Preface

Ordinarily a preface is placed at the beginning of a book—where no one reads it. We decided to sneak it in after the first chapter because we felt that it is important that the student understand where he is going. This "Preface" then, is a roadmap for the course.

As was pointed out in the first chapter, EDP began with the Univac I in 1954. Although the term "data processing" had been used before that, there were no jobs specifically requiring a knowledge of the subject. The computer did eliminate some routine bookkeeping and accounting jobs, but in less than ten years it also created hundreds of other opportunities. This is analogous to the invention of the automobile; although it eliminated or reduced job opportunities for buggy-whip manufacturers and horseshoers, it created thousands of jobs, directly, as in the manufacture of cars and their servicing, and also indirectly, as in roadbuilding and motel operation.

In this first course in data processing, you will get a survey of the field of business data processing. You will also be taught how data processing fits into the operation of a business and you will gain an understanding of terms and techniques. You will learn what machines are used, what they can do, and how they operate.

The first chapter explained what data processing is. In the next chapter, we will show how data are used in business. The third chapter, on the history of data processing, is intended to show that our subject is a dynamic, flexible one, and that today's methods may become obsolete tomorrow. Nevertheless, the emphasis on fundamentals in the first two chapters will enable the student to grasp quickly any new technique that is developed. Chapter 4 describes methods of manual and machine data processing and their applications.

11

The second part of the book covers in detail the special type of machine data processing which uses punched cards like the familiar IBM card. Machines using these cards have been designed for almost every business function. A system using only these machines is complete in itself and is known as punched-card data processing. Even when a computer is used, some punched-card machines are usually required as auxiliary equipment.

The rest of the book goes into computer data processing in more detail. We learn how to "talk" to the computer and how to understand the computer's output, how to organize the flow of data into and out of a computer, and how this flow fits into the general flow of data in a business.

The student majoring in data processing will eventually be qualified for many types of positions in this field. These include sophisticated programming and flow charting, manufacturing control, production control, cost accounting, systems analysis, operations research, and many others, including many important management jobs. An interesting fringe benefit of the data-processing curriculum is that a knowledge of data flow in business gives one the ability to handle many management jobs more efficiently, even in a business which does not use a computer.

In the first chapter it was indicated that executives and managers must have some knowledge of BDP because of the increased use of computers in industry. In addition, this first course is important in the curriculum of economists, accountants, and *everyone who keeps records*. A simple example of the advantages to be gained from a computer is the operation of a prescription pharmacy. Besides the usual bookkeeping and inventory functions, the computer can be used to keep track of prescriptions. Ordinarily, prescriptions are assigned numbers as they are received and are filed numerically. If the customer loses the number and wants the prescription renewed, it may take hours to locate the prescription in the file. With a computer, the prescription is filed in the memory storage and can be recalled by number, customer's name, or principal ingredient in a fraction of a second.

When you approach this subject, it is important for you, the reader, to understand that we are not dealing with a mysterious, secret business. As each topic is presented, try to imagine how it can be used or how it is applicable in a small shop, such as the local pharmacy, bakery, or hardware store. Besides helping to dispel the mystery, this practice aids in developing an understanding of data processing and its applications.

2

Data In Business

2–1 BUSINESS DATA

In the happy days before income taxes were invented, it was possible for a man to operate a business without keeping any records. He could buy and sell strictly for cash, and whether or not he made a profit was of no concern to the government or anyone else. Thus, a furniture maker could run a one-man independent business. He would buy his supplies and materials at the lumber yard and hardware store and pay cash. In his shop he would build a desk or table and chairs, for example, and then sell the articles to local customers, who in turn paid cash as they received the furniture. During the time between the purchase of materials and the sale of the furniture, he would probably spend money for food and other necessities, and if he ended with as much money as when he began, he would probably figure he had done well.

However, if business improves, our furniture maker may find it necessary to keep track of facts concerned with the business. If he has several orders, he will find it cheaper to buy supplies in larger quantities. He may lack the funds to pay for everything at once, but on the strength of his orders he can easily buy on credit. His customers, also, may prefer to pay their bills at some later date, so that our furniture maker must keep track of what is owed him and by whom. His store of supplies and materials will have to be replenished as business increases. Thus, he will have to know what he has on hand and, from this, deduce what he must purchase to complete the orders on the books. These *facts* concerned with the operation of the business are what we mean by *business data*.

2–2 CREATION OF NEW DATA

Any business, even a simple one-man cash business, generates or creates business data. Thus, when our furniture maker bought a sheet of plywood and paid cash for it, the facts exist that he made a purchase and

13

paid a certain sum. In this simple, pretax business it was not necessary to record or manipulate the facts in any manner, so the data were not *processed*. However, they could have been, if anyone were interested. (Of course, in today's economy, they would be processed, since the tax collector is interested, if no one else.) There are nine operations which create new data or affect the flow or organization of data in a business. These operations are the same for a large, complex business as they are for the elementary business described at the beginning of this chapter. Only the methods of processing the facts have improved. The nine operations are purchasing, receiving, inventory, production, selling, delivery, billing, collecting, and disbursing.

As we saw, the furniture maker had to buy lumber. This is *purchasing*. In any business, it is necessary to buy the raw materials which go into the finished product, but in a larger business, it is also necessary to buy many other things such as office supplies, delivery trucks, janitorial service, and possibly even lawn seed for the front lawn. Anything that is bought is included in purchasing.

In most businesses, ordering or purchasing is done by telephone or mail, and the material or service is delivered later. When the material arrives, it is *received*. It must be checked to ascertain that what was received (whether goods or service) agrees with what was ordered.

Goods or materials which have been received become part of the *inventory* or stock of supplies. Since this stock is continually changing, there must be some method of ensuring that the inventory meets current needs. This is called *maintaining the inventory*. In a small store, the owner may maintain his inventory simply by ordering a new supply of any item whenever he has only two of that item left. In larger businesses, there may be a need for having a continuing knowledge of how many of each item are in stock. It may be desirable to check this periodically by counting everything in stock. This is called *taking inventory*.

Production is the act of making the product which is to be sold. This may be an actual product such as a desk, auto, or loaf of bread or it may be a service such as gardening or window washing.

The finished product or service must be sold to a customer. It should be noted that *selling* may occur before production as well as after. Thus, our furniture maker may build a table and try to find a customer or he may build to order. Most *services* are usually sold first and "produced" later.

It is necessary to *deliver* the product or service. *Delivery* may occur simultaneously with selling, as when a loaf of bread is bought at the grocery. It may occur simultaneously with production, as when a gardener plants a tree.

Since many transactions are not paid for immediately, it becomes necessary to notify the customer that he owes money. This is usually done by sending a *bill*. *Billing* usually follows delivery, although in some transactions, billing and payment are made in advance.

In a reasonable time after the customer has received a bill, he will pay, usually by check or cash. The process of receiving the money is called *collecting*. Collecting also includes the steps taken to remind delinquent customers that they have not paid their bills.

After receiving money for delivery of goods or service, the business can now pay its own bills and expenses. The process of paying out is called *disbursing*. This includes payments to other businesses for materials and services as well as paychecks for employees and even charitable contributions.

The nine functions above are interrelated. For example, if raw materials are bought (purchasing), they must be accepted when they are shipped (receiving). Then they must be paid for (disbursing). Similarly when goods are sold (selling), they must be shipped to the customer (delivery). In due time, the customer is reminded that he owes money (billing), and he pays (collecting). It is also apparent that production is related to the number of orders, and inventory is affected by production, delivery, and sales. Each function creates data or business facts every time it operates, and because of the interrelation, the facts are utilized in other functions.

2–3 EXAMPLE

Let us consider a clothing manufacturer, the ABC Company. Their salesmen have been unusually successful so that they have a large number of orders. The orders are checked against the raw materials in stock, and it is found that about 500 more buttons will be needed. Anticipating more orders, the buyer for the ABC Company purchases 2000 buttons from the XYZ Buttons and Bows Company in the same city. The purchase order, stating colors and types of buttons, is mailed, and the buttons are delivered from stock by an errand boy, who presents a receipt to be signed by someone in the ABC Company. Later that month, the ABC Company buys 100 bows from the XYZ Company, as well as other items from other companies. At the end of the month, the XYZ Company sends the ABC Company a bill for the 2000 buttons and 100 bows.

The XYZ Buttons and Bows Company obviously has been affected by the increased sales of the ABC Company. However, from the standpoint of data processing, it is interested only in the movement of data within its own plant, i.e., the two different orders from the ABC Com-

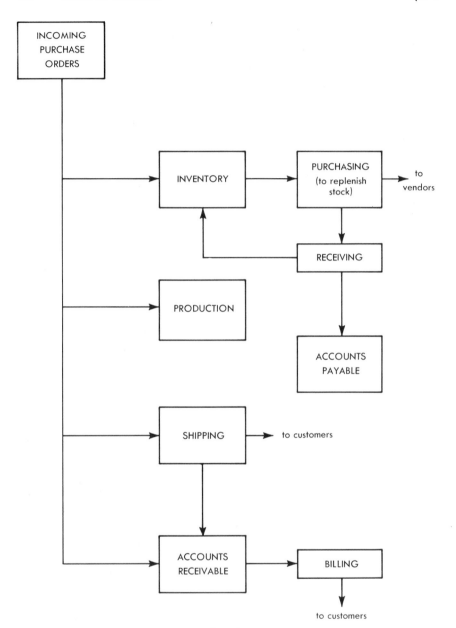

Fig. 2-1. Flow chart for ABC Company.

pany. Even though ABC came to XYZ, so far as XYZ is concerned, this is selling. The XYZ Company shipped or delivered the items out of its stock or inventory. The inventory list was adjusted and perhaps, if the supply of buttons was now low, production was started to replenish the stock. At the end of the month, the XYZ Company billed the ABC Company. To avoid having to run through the month's transactions to make sure that every ABC purchase is on the bill, XYZ maintains a separate record for each customer. As each order is received, it is recorded in the customer's account as well as being checked against inventory and presented to the shipping department for delivery.

It should be noted that the functions in the ABC Company are also related to functions in the XYZ Company. Thus, ABC's purchasing is XYZ's selling; XYZ's delivery is ABC's receiving; ABC's disbursing is XYZ's collecting.

In both companies, data were generated and then flowed from one department to another, sometimes generating more data. A *flow chart* shows how data are manipulated and flow in a business.

Figure 2-1 is a flow chart for the transactions mentioned above for the ABC Company. The information on the incoming purchase orders is checked against the inventory lists. Supplies are moved from stock to the production department, but this movement does not appear on the flow chart, which shows only the flow of data. As supplies are moved, the inventory lists are corrected, so that the lists are always current. When the inventory is low, reordering information is sent to purchasing. The purchase order data also go to the production department, so that the workers will know what to make; to shipping, so that the completed articles can be delivered to the proper customers as they are finished; and to the accounting department, where they are listed in accounts receivable for future billing. Note that the purchase orders generated data in inventory, in the form of corrected lists. Low stock in inventory generated data in purchasing, in the form of orders for buttons and bows. When these articles were purchased, received, and added to inventory, data flowed from receiving to correct the lists. The shipping department generated data whenever it filled an order. These data are sent to accounting so that bills will not be mailed until after goods are shipped. The data output of purchasing goes to the XYZ Company but it also flows to the receiving department. When the buttons are received, they are checked against the purchase, and then the data are sent to the accounting department, where they are listed in the accounts payable file for future disbursing.

Figure 2-2 is a flow chart for the XYZ Company. The orders from the ABC Company are checked against inventory, and the required buttons and bows are transferred to the shipping department. The inventory

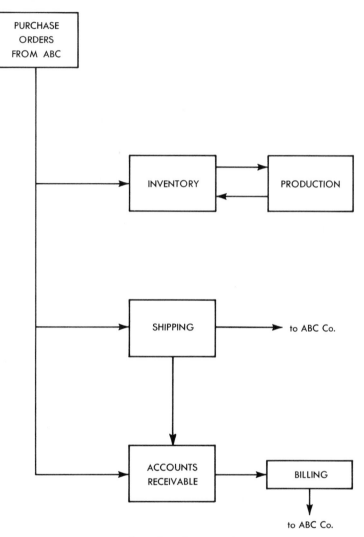

FIG. 2-2. Flow chart for XYZ Company.

lists are corrected, and when they indicate the need, data are sent to production to replenish the stock. When the stock is corrected, the information flows back from production to inventory to make the lists current. The information on the purchase orders also goes to shipping and accounts receivable, as in the case of the ABC Company. When the errand boy brings back the signed receipt, this information goes to the accounting department. This again is a precaution against billing before delivery.

2–4   MANIPULATION OF DATA

The manipulation, utilization, and creation of data in business generally
fall into six categories. These are recording, classifying, sorting, calculating, summarizing, and communicating. None of these were necessary in the one-man pretax business, but usually all six are necessary in
even the simplest business today.

When a *record* is made of any data, this is *recording*. Thus the list of
stock in inventory is a record. As inventory increases or decreases the
changes are recorded. In the ABC Company, data on incoming orders
were recorded in shipping and accounts receivable, so that later the data
could be used to indicate where to ship the order and when to send the
bill.

The data cannot be recorded just anywhere, but must be *classified*
according to their use. Thus, the incoming orders above are recorded in
accounts receivable and never in accounts payable. Classifying is also
called *coding*.

Within a given classification there may be further division. Thus, in
accounts receivable there are several customers listed in some systematic
manner, perhaps alphabetically. The process of listing systematically is
called *sorting*. The *sort* may be alphabetical, numerical, chronological,
or any other arrangement, but it is simply a filing system within a classification or category.

There is always some arithmetic connected with business. *Calculating*
is the process of using arithmetic manipulations. For example, to calculate
their bill to the ABC Company, the XYZ Company had to multiply 2000
by the price of a button and 100 by the price of a bow and add the two
products. Other obvious calculations in business are used to determine
paychecks, bank interest, etc.

It is usually necessary or desirable to *summarize* the information at
hand in a condensed form. Thus the ABC Company needs to know how
large its backlog of orders is, so that it can maintain a store of supplies.
This process involves taking the data from the incoming purchase orders
and summing the information; i.e., it consists of both calculating and
summarizing. Similarly, a summary may show the total amount owed to
or by a company or the profit or loss from operations. The bill from the
XYZ Company to the ABC Company is a summary of the latter's purchases during the month.

The flow charts in Figs. 2-1 and 2-2 show that data must move from
one department to another in a company. That is, it is necessary to
communicate data. The billing department, for instance, must be made
aware of deliveries so that bills will be sent. In the one-man business,
communication was unnecessary, since the proprietor had all the informa-

tion. In any larger business, communication is necessary to avoid duplication or omission.

Data processing consists of these six manipulations. From the moment a new element of business data is entered until its closing entry (for example, bill is marked "paid"), this element is processed. It should be emphasized that data processing is nothing more than this. The six parts of data processing, again, are recording, classifying or coding, sorting, calculating, summarizing, and communicating.

BIBLIOGRAPHY

MOORE BUSINESS FORMS, INC., *Forms for the 9 Key Operations of Business,* MI-120. The nine key business operations are enumerated and defined, and forms associated with each of these operations are illustrated. This booklet is an excellent introduction to our subject.

QUESTIONS

2–1
What is one of the main reasons why the volume of data processing has increased so much?

2–2
What are the nine basic operations that either create new data or affect the flow or organization of data in a business?

2–3
How can business data processing be applied to improve the inventory function of a business?

2–4
What are examples of business data related to the selling or marketing operation of a business that might be recorded or processed?

2–5
What is meant by the *disbursing* function or operation of a business?

2–6
What are the implications that distinguish the term *billing* from the term *collecting?*

2–7
What are the six categories of creating, using, and manipulating data?

2–8
What is the relationship between classifying and sorting data?

2–9

Assume that you have a file of 10,000 sales slips from a department store. The data on each sales slip are *classified* according to salesman, number, branch number, department number, kind of merchandise, number of items purchased, color, size, and dollar sales amount. What are some of the ways in which the data from these 10,000 sales slips could be *sorted?*

2–10

What distinctions can you make between the terms *calculating* and *summarizing?*

2–11

How can business data processing equipment help in the *communicating* phase of a business operation?

3

History of Data Processing

3-1 EARLY CALCULATORS

The nine business operations related to data flow, described in Chapter 2, are the same today as they were a thousand years ago. The methods of manipulating the data, however, have changed drastically and are continually changing. A history of data processing is simply a story of the development of methods of manipulation, which depend specifically on methods of computation.

When man first had to keep track of his possessions, he had to invent numbers so that he could count. Presumably, because he had ten fingers and it was easy to perform simple calculations by counting on fingers, man developed a numbering system (or counting system) based on the number *ten*. This is called the *decimal system*. Several different numbering systems with other bases have also been tried, but the decimal system became universal and survived.

As "business" developed, transactions involved more complicated counting. To facilitate this, man made marks on the ground or used stones and sticks for arithmetic. For transactions involving future payment it was necessary to keep records. This was done by making marks on wax or stone. Later, to avoid losing his counting stones he used beads on a string, which then developed into the abacus, a device still in use today. It is possible to multiply using an abacus, but the process involves mental processes as well as manipulation of the beads. To "automate" multiplication, that is, to remove the need for thinking, John Napier (1617) invented what was basically a three-dimensional abacus, using rods instead of beads. This device came to be known as *Napier's bones* and was the forerunner of the slide rule.

The abacus had been in existence for more than 3000 years before the first improvement in calculating devices appeared, but after Napier's bones, new inventions appeared quickly. In 1642, Blaise Pascal invented an adding machine using ten-toothed numbered wheels. His basic principle is still used in electric desk-type calculators. Samuel Morland in 1666 extended Pascal's machine to perform subtraction as well as addition. Gottfried Leibnitz in 1694 improved on Morland's machine with one that could also multiply, divide, and take square roots. All of these machines, however, were unreliable because of inadequate technology. During the next two centuries, emphasis was placed on improving reliability and production methods, and in 1885 the first successful key-operated calculator was put on the market.

Near the close of the eighteenth century, an invention appeared which had nothing to do with counting or calculating, but which had a tremendous impact on the future of data processing. Joseph Jacquard invented a method of controlling a weaving loom by means of a punched card. The position of the holes determined the pattern. Later Herman Hollerith adapted the punched card to control an adding machine. (The punched cards used by IBM still employ the *Hollerith code*.) About 1835, Charles Babbage conceived of a device (which he called an *analytical engine*) that would use a sequence of punched cards to perform a long computation. His machine was never built but his ideas were later used in the first electronic computers.

Before discussing computers, we should note that these inventions did not eliminate the human from the processing chain; they merely simplified an existing operation so that it could be performed with less effort, more speed, and greater reliability. Just as the abacus extended the ability to solve arithmetic problems, so the modern computers extend the human functions to solve more complex problems. If it were not for the computers, many of these problems would never be undertaken, because of lack of sufficient manpower to solve them or the impossibility of getting a solution in time to be effective. An example of the former is the dial telephone, mentioned in Chapter 1. An example of the latter, in the field of warfare, is the ability to calculate the firing position of antiaircraft guns when an enemy plane approaches. The computer receives the information on speed and position of the enemy plane, direction of wind, and anything else that might affect the accuracy of the shot, and automatically positions and fires the guns. The calculations could be performed by humans, but not before the approaching plane had completed its destructive mission.

The abacus, adding machines, desk calculators, and the like were not invented as "business" machines, but rather as devices to simplify arithmetic. It was only logical that the more advanced calculators would be combined with typewriters to make *business machines* in the real sense, machines equipped to perform specific bookkeeping functions.

These are the mechanical or electromechanical data-processing machines. In manual data processing, bookkeeping functions are performed by hand, although some calculations may be performed on an electric calculator. Machine data processing makes use of business machines to perform the calculations and record the results in the proper files automatically. For example, the business machine used by hotels furnishes an itemized bill for each guest. When the bill is paid, the machine receipts the bill, and at the same time records the amount. The total receipts for a day, week, or longer period are also recorded.

The first electronic computers were not designed as business data processors, but rather as machines to solve very complicated mathematical problems. Just as the abacus and desk caculator were adopted by business, so also was the computer. And just as a combination of existing machines, the calculator and typewriter, made a machine specifically designed for business problems, so electronic computers were combined with other equipment to make special business computers. The difference between a business computer and one designed to solve engineering or mathematical problems lies in the capacities of its component parts. A business computer must be capable of receiving vast quantities of data, on which it must perform relatively simple arithmetic, and then it must print out vast quantities of data. For example, the payroll function of a large factory requires nothing more complicated than multiplication (hours times payrate) and subtraction (deduct taxes), but this has to be done for thousands of employees. On the other hand, a mathematical problem may require very little input and output but have many complicated steps in the solution.

3–2 DEVELOPMENT OF THE MODERN COMPUTER

The forerunner of the modern electronic computer was a machine called Mark I, built by IBM and Harvard University in 1944. This machine incorporated Babbage's ideas and was built primarily to compute ballistic firing tables. Since it used relays for switches, the speed was limited. It could perform about three additions per second—amazingly fast at the time—but was far short of the 250,000 additions per second achieved on later electronic machines.

The first large-scale *electronic* computer was built in 1945 and called ENIAC, for *E*lectronic *N*umber *I*ntegrator *A*nd *C*omputer. It contained almost 20,000 tubes and required about 150,000 watts of power to operate. About 40,000 watts was required simply to drive fans to cool the tubes. It was built by the Moore School of Electrical Engineering at the University of Pennsylvania for the Army Ordnance Department. ENIAC was retired in 1958 because, compared to newer computers, it was too expensive to operate. Computers with names like EDVAC, SEAC, UNIVAC, etc., appeared in rapid succession after the ENIAC in 1945. Each new computer utilized the latest technology to produce greater speed or greater reliability, as well as greater capacity. For example, the ENIAC was plagued with tube failures, but the EDVAC used germanium diodes in place of some of the tubes. In 1952, RCA produced a storage unit for a computer, using tiny ferrite cores about the size of a printed letter "O" in this book. The cores were cheap, easily produced, and had indefinite life. Meanwhile, the transistor had been developed in 1948 and although its acceptance had been slow, in 1957 IBM introduced the 1620 computer, which was the first all solid-state computer. That is, it used transistors and magnetic cores throughout and had no tubes at all. Although built primarily for scientific calculations, the 1620 also could be used in the new field of business data processing which the UNIVAC opened in 1954.

It should be noted that the computers used in electronic data processing belong to the class of *digital* computers. That is, they solve problems by using digits, or numbers, and arithmetic calculations. The other class is the *analog* computer, which solves problems by some physical analogy to the problem rather than by counting. The analog computer is especially suited to some scientific problems and is not used for business data processing; the *digital* computer has application in both fields.

The digital computer, as its name implies, supplies answers in digital form, that is, using numbers. An analog computer, however, derives answers from differences in voltage or other physical "analogies." In calculating the trajectory of a ballistic missile, for example, the output of an analog computer is a smooth trace of the path taken by the missile. In contrast, the output of the digital computer is simply a series of numbers which describe a series of points on the missile's path. If these points are close enough together, then, of course, the whole trajectory can be determined by drawing a smooth curve through the points. In business data processing, where answers are wanted in digital form, the digital computer is better suited to the task.

New technological developments are adopted by the computer industry to produce machines that are smaller, faster, cheaper, more accurate and more versatile. Although the basic business operations do not change, the computer has affected the methods of doing business. The techniques of linear programming and critical path analysis mentioned in Chapter 1 enable managers to make better decisions. If the company president is wondering whether to open a branch office in another state, he can supply the computer with all the relevant data, such as starting costs, overhead costs, salaries, minimum expected sales, typical difficulties (strikes, material shortages, etc.). The computer can then be run through months of business operation in a matter of seconds to show whether the office would be profitable or when it would begin to show a profit. This is called a computer *simulation* or *model* of the business, and is a technique which is frequently a combination of linear programming and critical path analysis.

Computers have enabled banks to compete more effectively with savings and loan organizations. The interest rate which banks are permitted to pay on deposit is limited by law, but there is no limit to how often the interest may be compounded. There is no restriction on interest paid by savings and loan organizations. Before they adopted computers, competitive banks compounded interest quarterly, requiring about ten days to calculate the interest at each quarter. Computers now enable them to pay interest daily.

The computer's advantages have been presented at length here and in Chapter 1, but there are disadvantages, also. The initial cost of equipment is high. This must be weighed against the expected savings or gain. The initial cost of programming the machine is also high. However, these costs are decreasing. Since the machine is expensive, a company rarely can afford more than one computer. This means that management must plan computer activity carefully so that maximum use is made of it.

BIBLIOGRAPHY

BABBAGE, HENRY P., ED., *Babbage's Calculating Engines.* London: E. and F. N. Spon, 1889. This early book presents a thorough description of Babbage's original contributions to automatic computers.

BOWDEN, B. V., *Faster Than Thought.* London: Pitman and Sons, Ltd., 1953. This book is a general introduction to the operation and structure of electronic digital computing machines.

GRAY, H. J., *Digital Computer Engineering.* Englewood Cliffs, N. J.: Prentice-Hall, Inc., 1963. The first chapter of this book is a fair summary of computer history. The rest of the book is written primarily for engineering students.

MORRISON, PHILIP and EMILY, "The Strange Life of Charles Babbage," *Scientific American,* April 1952, pp. 66–73. This is an interesting biography of Charles Babbage and discussion of his contributions.

The student should read "The Strange Life of Charles Babbage" and the first chapter of *Digital Computer Engineering.* The other references are optional.

QUESTIONS

3–1
What contribution did John Napier make to data processing?

3–2
Who invented the first machine that used punched cards to control its operation? What was accomplished by using the punched cards?

3–3
What were the main difficulties of the early "data-processing" machines that limited their usefulness?

3–4
What is it that distinguishes a business data-processing computer from a computer used in science, engineering or mathematical applications?

3–5
What was the first large-scale electronic computer?

3–6
There are two basic kinds of computers. What are they and in what fields are they used?

3–7
The name of Herman Hollerith is very significant in the field of business data processing. What can you find through your research efforts, concerning his contributions to business data processing?

3–8
What is meant by a "model" of a business operation?

3–9
What are some of the disadvantages of installing and using a computer in business data processing?

4

Manual and Machine Data Processing

4–1 MANUAL DATA PROCESSING

When all the record-keeping and bookkeeping operations of a business are done by hand, the business is using *manual* data processing. The nine business operations, described in Chapter 2, generate data which are frequently used in several of the other operations. In order to avoid repetitive copying of records, a sufficient number of carbon copies are made of all records which are needed in more than one place. These may be typed or handwritten. All entries in account books are made by hand, although some of the arithmetic may be performed on a desk calculator or adding machine.

As an example, let us consider Jim's Janitorial Service, which uses manual data processing. Jim employs two girls who do secretarial and bookkeeping work, a stock boy, and fifteen to twenty cleaners, depending on the volume of business. The company furnishes cleaning services for other businesses on contract. When a prospective customer applies for cleaning service, Jim visits the customer's plant or business, and he and the customer agree on the frequency and amount of service necessary. After calculating the cost, Jim supplies two standard contract forms which are signed by both. One copy is left with the customer and Jim keeps the other.

When he returns to his office, Jim hands the contract to one of the secretaries who then *opens an account* for the new customer. This consists of typing the customer's name and address at the top of a large card. She then adds other information, such as which cleaning men are assigned to the job and what days or how frequently they will clean. In order to have money coming in evenly during the month, customers are not all billed on the same day but are billed randomly. The secretary assigns a billing date, for example, the 15th of each month, which she also types on the card. The rest of the card has spaces for entering charges against the customer and for payments received. To avoid going through the complete list of customers to check when to send a bill, it is desirable to have a separate list of customers, arranged chronologically by billing date. The girl adds the new customer's name to this list in the space for the 15th of the month.

When the cleaners make their rounds, they perform the various cleaning tasks specified in the contracts and also replenish supplies of paper towels, toilet paper, and hand soap, for which the customer pays extra. When they return to Jim's Janitorial Service offices, they present a list of places visited and extra supplies used in each place. For payroll purposes and for analysis by accountants later, they also list the hours worked at each customer's establishment. The girls enter on the customer's cards the date the cleaners visited and the extra charges.

Each day the secretaries check their billing date lists to see which customers are to be billed. The large account cards are then pulled from the accounts receivable file (where they are sorted alphabetically) and bills are typed. Each bill lists the stipulated contract amount plus itemized extra charges for supplies. In figuring totals the girls use desk adding machines. When checks are received, the amounts are credited to the customers' accounts on their account cards, and the checks are deposited in Jim's bank account.

Each cleaning crew consists of a driver, who is also foreman of the crew, and two to four other workmen. From the lists which they return, the secretaries enter hours worked for each individual on that individual's work record. The weekly paycheck is calculated by multiplying a worker's hours by his hourly rate and subtracting the usual deductions for taxes, social security, health insurance, etc. Separate records are kept of total deductions so that Jim's Janitorial Service can pay accumulated taxes when due and divert other sums as needed. The men are paid weekly. Jim may sign each check individually or he may authorize a girl to sign for him or to use a special stamp. The hours spent at each job will also be recorded on the customer's account card so that later an accountant can determine which jobs (or perhaps, which types of jobs) are most profitable and which customers should be charged more.

The company maintains a stock of supplies needed for its business. This includes waxes, soaps, disinfectants, paper products, brooms, mops, sponges, etc. They also have spare floor waxers and vacuum cleaners. These are all kept in a stock room from which each foreman can draw supplies and machines as needed. The stock boy keeps a record of what is drawn and is responsible for reordering to maintain the inventory. He fills out all orders in triplicate. The original is sent to the vendor, one copy goes to a secretary, and he keeps the other. When he receives the supplies, he notes this on his copy of the order, which he then sends to the secretary. The first copy was entered in the record of expenses and "warned" the front office that a bill would be forthcoming. The second copy indicated that it was all right to pay the bill since the shipment had been received. Records of bills paid must be kept for tax purposes also.

Jim's Janitorial Service also has transactions involving truck maintenance, secretaries' salaries, insurance, and many other aspects of running a business. However, the above description of operations is sufficient to illustrate flow of data and manual data processing involving the nine business functions described in Chapter 2. When the contract is signed, Jim's Janitorial Service is involved in *selling*. Service is the commodity. Even though nothing has been delivered as yet, the fact that a new customer has been added must be recorded in accounts receivable (by preparing an account card) and in *billing* (by listing the customer according to billing date).

In this business, as with most service businesses, *production* and *delivery* are simultaneous. The data concerning each delivery must be transmitted to the proper places for future billing and also for *disbursing* (paying salaries of cleaners). The billing data will result in bills which will produce checks. This is *collecting*. The production also affects *inventory*. Whenever stock on hand of a particular item is below a set amount, the stock boy will reorder. This is *purchasing*. Data from purchasing must normally be transmitted to receiving, but in this case both functions are performed by the same person. However, even in this case, the stock boy does keep a record of his purchases so that he can check orders received. Data from both purchasing and receiving are sent to disbursing so that bills will be paid when they are received.

4–2 RECORDING OF MANUAL DATA

It should be noted that data are *recorded* on many occasions. This is a very important step, since without the record it is impossible to tell whether errors have been made in the *communication* of information. To simplify the recording of data it is common practice to design *forms* which can be filled in easily and which are usually self-explanatory. Thus the foreman of each cleaning crew could list all the pertinent facts of his crew's work on a blank piece of paper, but his job is simplified if he uses a form. A simple form for this chore is shown in Fig. 4-1. This form also simplifies the work of the secretaries, since the extra charges for a particular item will always appear in the same column in all reports.

The forms used in a business may be simple, standard items, such as sales slips or they may be designed especially for the job at hand, as the foreman's form of Fig. 4-1. In general, the person who can best design

Crew: _____	Foreman: _____	Date: _____
_____		
_____		
_____		
_____		

Customer	Hours worked	Supplies furnished		
		Towels	Toilet paper	Soap

FIG. 4-1. Form for recording data.

the form is the one who has to read the information from it. It is possible to overdo the practice of filling out forms, especially in a business using manual data processing, and in general, forms should not be forced into a situation where information is recorded adequately and is communicated efficiently. A common sense approach should be taken and forms should be used only if they simplify the communication of information.

In the business described, the *classification* problem is quite simple: the customers are accounts receivable, the vendors are accounts payable. The information on a foreman's report does require some classifying. Thus, the extra supplies must be translated to money (calculating) and posted to individual accounts for billing. Hours worked are transmitted to employees' accounts, where again they are translated to money for disbursing. The arithmetic calculations for both types of transaction are probably done on desk calculators. Thus the manipulation of data called *calculating* is done by machine even in manual data processing. In figuring paychecks for employees, one encounters many types of deductions. Two well-known deductions are those for income tax and social security. Since the company has to pay the deducted sums to the federal government, it is necessary to keep records of what has been deducted and from whose paycheck. The classification "deductions" may be sub-classified into "income tax" and "social security." The total amount paid for each is a *summary* of that deduction. Similarly, other useful summaries are total wages paid, total utility bills, total receipts, etc.

When checks are received from customers, individual accounts must be credited. It is usual to make a list of amounts received and deposit the checks immediately. At some convenient time, amounts on the list are posted as credits to the proper customer cards. Since the account cards are usually arranged alphabetically, it is desirable to *sort* the amounts on the list in the same manner to simplify the posting procedure. In a small company, manual sorting is simple, no matter how it is done, but in a large company with many customers, sorting techniques can be important. Suppose a company has 10,000 customers (a utility, for example), and the account cards for these customers are arranged alphabetically. If 100 new customers are added, it follows that 100 new account cards must be *collated* with the 10,000 (that is, interleaved in the proper places) to maintain the alphabetic order. It is possible to pick up each of the 100 new cards and locate its proper place in the old deck of 10,000. However, it may be quicker to arrange the 100 new cards alphabetically first, even though it means an additional step. Likewise, in sorting the 100 cards, an additional step of dealing them into separate piles (an *A* pile, a *B* pile, etc.) may result in a faster sort.

Before someone coined the term "data processing" we probably would have referred to the six manipulations of data in Jim's Janitorial Service as *bookkeeping*. Bookkeepers recorded data. They had to know where to record the items, and this is classifying. The classification was always sorted, usually alphabetically. They calculated paychecks, dis-counts, and performed other routine business computations. The totals of columns or classifications were summaries. Finally, they communicated the information to the proper individuals for action. Thus a bookkeeper in a small company is a data processor just as much as the computer operators in a large company.

4–3 MACHINE DATA PROCESSING

In the operation of Jim's Janitorial Service we saw that when the foreman of a crew turned in his list of jobs performed, the bookkeepers had to copy the relevant data onto the customers' account cards. This is called *posting*. In this case the bookkeepers post some of the data to accounts receivable and some to payroll. Similarly, the information about orders to vendors is posted to accounts payable. In some companies, a single transaction may result in posting to many different accounts. In the course of copying information, errors can arise (such as writing 14 instead of 41, etc). To eliminate the possibility of errors in copying and to reduce the number of transcriptions necessary, it is desirable to have a system where the information or data are posted automatically when written only once. A simple and obvious solution is to use carbon copies. Thus, when the stock boy in Jim's Janitorial Service orders supplies, he makes carbon copies for internal records instead of copying the order sheet over again.

When Jim's bookkeeper wanted to send a bill, she pulled out the customer's account card and copied the pertinent data on a bill form. Again, the operation would be simplified if the original information from the foreman's list were entered on both a bill form and the customer's account card at the same time by using carbon paper. In this case, since the bill and the account card are different sizes, it is necessary to align them and the carbon paper carefully.

In a larger operation, the information on a sales slip or other form may require posting to many accounts. For example, in a department store a clerk sells a dress to a charge customer. The data on the sales slip are posted to the customer's account in accounts receivable, to the clerk's account in payroll (to compute her commission), to the customer's bill, to the record of daily sales, to inventory control, and perhaps others. In an automatic posting system, the bookkeepers could enter the transaction once and it would appear in all the right places immediately. This can be done by pulling out all the proper forms, interleaving them with carbon paper, and aligning them carefully—since they are probably of different sizes. A simple contraption called a *peg board* or *posting board* is used to solve the alignment problem. This is simply a board with pegs or other means of holding prepunched forms in proper alignment. To simplify the interleaving problem it is also possible to buy forms already interleaved in any desired arrangements.

The posting board is not a "machine" in the accepted sense, but it is sometimes considered to be a form of machine data processing because it eliminates hand copying. At what point "manual" becomes "machine" seems to be a matter of familiarity. Thus, when adding machines were first introduced, their use was considered machine bookkeeping. The typewriter and adding machine today are considered accessories for manual data processing, but many business machines used in machine data processing are nothing more than combinations of typewriters and adding machines.

One of the first machines for data processing was the cash register. It should be noted that the money drawer on the cash register is incidental and is not the prime purpose of the machine. The cash register records transactions involving cash. The original registers recorded individual transactions and presented a sum of the cash received. Buttons were added to code the transactions for individual clerks or separate departments. Thus, a supermarket manager, for example, had a running total of receipts for meat, fruits, etc., as well as of the receipts taken in by each clerk. In ringing up sales, clerks can take subtotals on taxable items. Some registers even calculate the tax and automatically figure the change due the customer. Basically, the cash register is simply an adding machine or group of adding machines.

The first adding machines, calculators, and cash registers were completely mechanical, requiring the user to turn a crank to operate them. Later the crank was replaced by an electric motor, and the result was an electromechanical machine. Some of the newer calculators are electronic with no moving parts. They are faster, quieter, and require less maintenance than the electromechanical machines.

4–4 PROGRAMS

An accounting machine or business machine is simply a combination of a typewriter and cash register (or adding machine). Forms are placed into the machine in proper alignment or in different places in the same machine. When an item is entered (by typewriter or by pushing the adding machine buttons), the machine prints the proper information and enters totals in the proper places on all the forms. During the printing process, the machine shifts the platen or roller containing the forms so that the printing can occur at the correct spot on each form. In an ordinary typewriter there are stops, called tabulators, which the typist can set to predetermined positions on the roller. Then when she presses the tabulator key, the platen shifts to the next stop automatically. The business machine also has tabulators, but they shift the carriage not only from left to right but also from top to bottom. An arrangement of these stops for a given job is called a *program,* and some machines can make as many as 25 entries from one typing. That is, the operator types in the item and pushes the start button. The machine then prints the item, or totals dependent on it, in 25 different places on assorted pieces of paper. Some machines have split platens. That is, the roller is divided in two at the center, and the left half turns at a different speed from the right half. When a machine is used for two or more different kinds of business functions (for example, payroll and billing), the program for one function may be quite different from another. It is possible to rearrange the stops that were just used in a billing program so that the machine can now be used for payroll. However, since the machine will be used for billing again at a later date, it is preferable to save the program. In some machines the stops are set on a removable bar so that it is possible to change programs by merely changing the bar. In this way, the original program is not destroyed.

Figure 4-2 is a photograph of an accounting machine built by National Cash Register and named Model 33. This is basically a combination of a typewriter and 21 adding machines. In a typical example this machine would be used to prepare *Form 914* for tax purposes. This is the tax form which a company files every three months, showing earnings of all employees and deductions withheld for social security, federal taxes, state unemployment, and a few other things.

FIG. 4-2. NCR Model 33. (Courtesy of National Cash Register Co.)

The amount of gross income on which an employee pays the social security tax is limited (it began at $3000 in 1937 and has been increasing ever since). Similarly, other deductions and taxes which the employer pays are limited. If an employee earns less than the limit, his whole salary is taxed; if more, the deduction is made only on the limit. Thus, in 1965, for example, social security deductions are made on the first $4800, federal unemployment tax (paid by employer) on the first $3000, and state unemployment (varies in each state) may be based on the first $4000. The 33 is programmed by adjusting the stops in the program bar to prepare Form 914. The operator simply types in each employee's name, social security number, and total salary. The machine then types the rest in the proper columns. For example, suppose that an employee has earned $6000. This is typed in the column marked "total earnings" by the operator. The machine also types $6000 in the column headed "earnings for federal income tax." It types $4800 in the column for "social security," $3000 in the "federal unemployment tax" column, and $4000 in the "state" column. If the employee earned only $3500, the three amounts would be $3500, $3000, and $3500. When the whole list is finished, the operator presses a button, and the machine prints the total of each column at the bottom of the column.

Let us return to Jim's Janitorial Service and see how an accounting machine would handle payroll. A check must be typed for each employee, and in addition, information must be recorded in a payroll summary journal, a check register, a record of earnings for the particular employee, and a pay statement for the employee. The payroll summary journal is a list of all payroll checks, arranged chronologically, giving names of the employees, earnings, deductions, net amounts of checks, and check numbers. The check register simply supplies the check numbers serially, not only for payroll, but for all disbursements. The record of the employee's earnings is a list of all the earnings, deductions, and net amounts the employee has received. The pay statement is given to the employee with his check and shows how the amount on the check was calculated. The payroll summary and check register are locked into the machine. For each employee, the typist inserts the employee's earning record card, a blank check, and a blank pay statement. On the cash register (or adding machine) part of the accounting machine, she punches in the last totals on the employee's earning record. She now types his name and his new earnings and deductions in the columns of the payroll journal. Then at the touch of a button the machine does the rest. It gets a number from the check register and types it on all the forms in the proper places. It enters the employee's name on his check and pay statement. It lists earnings, deductions, and net amount on the pay statement and also prints the net amount on the check. On the earnings record it prints the same information which was printed on the pay statement, plus accumulated totals, such as earnings to date, taxes withheld to date, etc. In jumping from one place on the forms to another, the machine follows the program determined by the tabulator stops. As long as the machine is used for payroll, the same program is used.

The same machine, with a different program can be used for billing. Let us go back to the XYZ Buttons and Bows Company, mentioned in Chapter 2. The XYZ Company receives orders, which it fills immediately from stock. Bills are sent monthly, but each customer may have received several orders since the last billing date. When an order is received, it is recorded in a journal, which is a summary of all orders received. When shipment is made, this is entered in the proper column in the same journal. The order and date of shipment are now recorded on the customer's card in accounts receivable. This lists amounts owed to the XYZ Company and payments made. In addition, checks received from customers must be recorded in a cash receipts journal, as well as credited to the customers' accounts. To record orders that have been shipped, the order summary journal is locked in the machine. A bill form with the customer's name and address on it and his account card are placed on the carriage, and the typist types the customer's name and the amount due on his shipment in the proper place in the summary journal. She also enters the balance shown on the bill, using the cash register part of the machine. Now when she pushes the start button, the information is printed on the bill and on the customer's account card, and the new balance is computed and appears on both. When checks are received, she locks the cash receipts journal in the machine instead of the order summary journal. The customer's bill and account card are placed on the carriage as before, and the balance is entered in the machine. Now when she types the data on the cash receipts journal and pushes the button, the information is recorded on the other two forms and the check is credited, making a new balance.

It should be apparent that forms for machine data processing are very important. In designing a form, one must consider the capabilities of the machine as well as the information to be recorded. It is possible to purchase forms made to special order for specific tasks. These can consist of bundles of interleaved sheets of different sizes as well as single sheets. As with manual data processing, the important consideration in the design of forms is ease of communicaton.

The business machines prevent errors caused by mistakes in copying when posting. Of course, the same can be said for the use of posting boards and carbon paper or for the use of duplicating machines. Business machines, however, also have the advantage of saving time by posting in many places with just one entry on the machine. However, it should be realized that these machines are doing exactly the same kind of data processing that was done manually. The data which are recorded, classified, sorted, operated on by calculating, summarized, and communicated in manual data processing go through the same manipulations in the same accounts and journals in machine data processing. The machine, however, requires less effort, is faster, and is not as likely to make a mistake.

Accounting machines have made data processing easier for the operators, but too often these operators have less knowledge of data processing than the bookkeepers who worked by hand. It is very easy to learn by rote which forms to put into the machine and which buttons to push. If you want to advance beyond the level of the machine operators, you must realize how the data are processed; that is, what the machine is doing.

BIBLIOGRAPHY

National Cash Register Co., *Equipment for the Total System*, SP-1514-A3RRR.

National Cash Register Co., *A Study of Machine Accounting Methods, Accounts Payable*, 1959.

National Cash Register Co., *A Study of Machine Accounting Methods, Accounts Receivable*, 1959.

National Cash Register Co., *A Study of Machine Accounting Methods, Payroll and Costs*, 1959.

QUESTIONS

4–1

Do the production and delivery functions of a business operation ever take place simultaneously? If so, when?

4–2

What is meant by purchasing in a business?

4–3

When the receiving clerk telephones the purchasing department to report that a certain shipment has arrived, which of the nine business operations is the receiving clerk performing?

4–4

Why do businesses use so many forms in their operations?

4–5

In the example of Jim's Janitorial Service used in this chapter, the data for the business were classified into accounts receivable and accounts payable. What other classifications of data can you think of that an owner or manager might wish to have in this business?

4–6

What is the advantage of using a peg board in data processing?

4–7

What is the difference between an electromechanical data-processing device and an electronic data-processing device?

4–8

What is the main advantage of using an accounting machine like the one in Fig. 4–2?

4–9

What is meant by the term collated?

4–10

Assume that you are establishing a new file system for your 10,000 customers. You want to be able to sort the file each month into alphabetical sequence. What would be one of the best ways to set up your file system regardless of whether you are going to process the file manually or use data-processing equipment?

PART 2

Punched Card Data Processing

5

Punched Cards

5-1 INTRODUCTION

It was pointed out in Chapter 3 that Herman Hollerith adapted the punched card feature of Jacquard's loom to control an adding machine. Herman Hollerith worked for the United States Census Bureau, and in 1890 his punched cards were used to count and tabulate. As a result, the 1890 census required only half the time required by that of 1880, despite a 20 percent increase in population over the decade. Hollerith's method was so successful that he left the Census Bureau and formed a company to build the necessary machines. This company eventually became the International Business Machines Corporation. The code used by IBM is still the old *Hollerith code,* although the card itself is somewhat different.

In 1911, another punched-card machine company entered the field. This company was later absorbed by what is now Sperry Rand Corporation, and their UNIVAC Division is still in the punched-card machine business. The UNIVAC card is the same size and shape as the IBM card, but uses a different code. In addition there are several smaller companies in this business, but most make equipment which is *compatible* with IBM equipment. That is, their punched cards can be used in IBM machines and vice versa. As a result, the IBM card is used in more than 80 percent of the punched-card equipment. The description of punched-card data processing in Chapters 5 through 7 will use the IBM card as a model, but the principles are general, and any kind of card with any kind of code could be the basis of a data-processing system.

Punched cards (also called *tab cards* or *IBM cards*) are important because they are a convenient form of input in electronic data-processing systems. In addition, it is possible to have a complete data-processing system using only punched cards and machines designed to handle them. This is called *punched card data processing.*

Each card is a *record* of a certain amount or type of information. A card may contain only one fact or as much as can be conveyed by 80 symbols, but in either case the card itself is considered a unit of information in the data-processing system. For this reason, the card is called a *unit record,* and the machines which process the cards are sometimes called *unit-record equipment.*

The idea of using a hole in a card to represent a fact is actually older than Jacquard's looms. (But the use of machines to read the cards and process the data is new.) Benjamin Franklin used holes in cards to classify the books in his large private collection. It should be noted that a hole or lack of it in a card is a *yes-no* decision. Thus, a hole at point *A* may represent that an object is red, a hole at point *B* may represent white, and one at point *C* may represent blue. Then, if there is a hole at point *B*, there must be no holes at *A* and *C*. In effect, we ask, "Is the object red?" and look at point *A* for the answer. There is no hole, so the answer is negative. We ask whether the object is white and find a hole to indicate that it is. Since there should be only one hole to represent a color, we can check that this is so by noting that there is no hole at *C*. This is a routine error check, since a second hole would indicate that an error has been made. In a similar manner, codes are frequently arranged so that an extra punch would indicate that an error has been made.

5–2 DESCRIPTION OF PUNCHED CARDS

Figure 5-1 shows an IBM card before it is punched. There are ten horizontal *rows,* from zero to nine, where punches can occur. In addition, punches can be located in two other horizontal rows which lie above the zero-row. The row nearest the top edge is called the *twelve*-row; the row between the twelve-row and the zero-row is called the *eleven*-row. (Sometimes the eleven- and twelve-rows are called *X*- and *Y*-rows, respectively.) The long edge of the card at the top is called the *twelve*-edge since the twelve-row is nearest to it; the bottom edge is the *nine*-edge. Each *column,* when punched, represents a single symbol. The symbol may be a letter of the alphabet, a number from zero to nine, or it may be a code for much more information or for an instruction to the machine. The punches in the zero- to nine-rows fall exactly on the digits. In the twelve- and eleven-rows the punches are lined up with those of the rows below. There are 80 columns, indicated by small digits at the bottom of the card and repeated between the zero- and one-rows. (There is a tendency to confuse *rows* and *columns.* A simple mnemonic aid is the fact that "columns" hold up buildings and thus must be vertical.)

The capacity of a card then is eighty symbols. In practice this is reduced by practical considerations. Thus, if the cards are to be used to describe

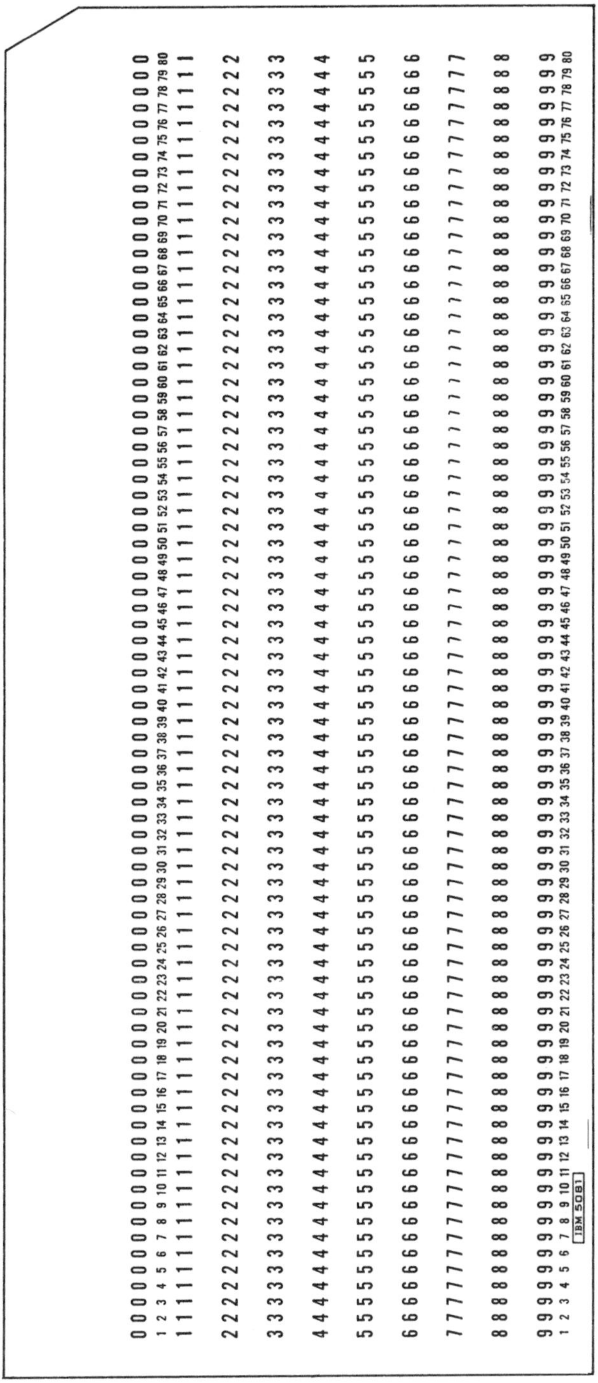

FIG. 5-1. IBM card blank.

people, the first twenty columns may be used for names, even though all names will not be the same length. The next three might be age, then three for weight, others for height, color of eyes, hair, etc. Each group of columns for a specific purpose is called a *field*. In our example, there would be a name field of twenty columns, an age field of three columns, and so on. It is necessary that a specific field be in the same position on all cards. Then when we want data on age, for example, our machine would scan only the age field (columns 21–23) and if required, could arrange the cards in order of increasing or decreasing age.

The IBM card is 0.007 inch thick. In general, the thicker a card is, the faster it can be processed. Thin cards are flimsy and need special care. The thickness chosen for the IBM card allows good speed without requiring excessive space for processing and storage.

The system of positions of holes in the card to represent characters is called a *code*. The holes in the rows from one through nine are called *numerical* punches. In the eleven- and twelve-rows, they are called *zone* punches. A hole in the zero-row with no other holes in the same column is a numerical punch, representing zero. If there are other holes in the same column, the zero punch is a zone punch. The IBM code for the digits from zero through nine and for the letters of the alphabet is shown in Fig. 5-2. Note that the holes are rectangular, about $\frac{1}{8}$ inch high and $\frac{1}{16}$ inch wide. By means of other combinations of two or three punches, it is possible to represent other characters such as dollar signs, mathematical symbols, punctuation marks, etc. To avoid weakening the card, no more than three punches are used in a column. The printed symbols at the top of the card indicate what has been punched. Some machines for punching cards print this information and punch simultaneously.

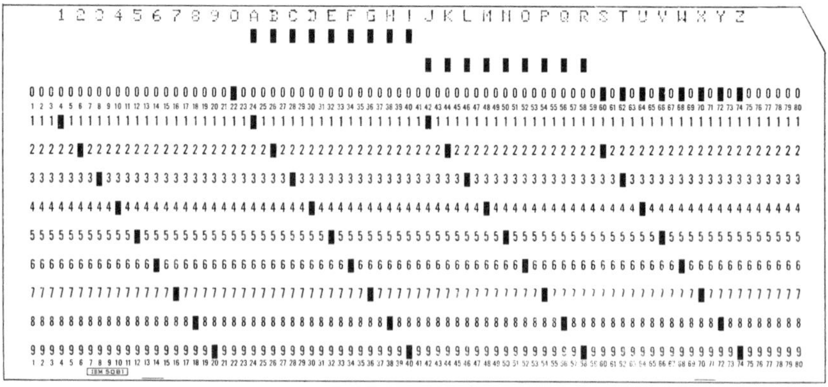

FIG. 5-2. IBM card punched.

Since the machines which process the information on the cards sense only the holes, it is obvious that the numbers printed on the face of the card shown in Fig. 5-1 are simply an aid to the operator. In most business data-processing applications, the printing on the card is more informative. Thus, if a card is used to represent a sale in a department store, the face of it may be divided into fields by vertical lines with headings such as "item purchased," "price," "clerk," etc. More common examples of IBM cards with special printing are paychecks of large concerns, telephone and gasoline bills, and refund checks from the Internal Revenue Service. In each case the punched holes and the *corner cut* identify it as an IBM card.

A small triangular piece is removed from the upper left-hand or upper right-hand corner of the card, as shown in Figs. 5-1 and 5-2. This is called a *corner cut* and is simply a visual aid for the operator which enables him to ascertain quickly that all cards are facing in the same direction and none are upside down. Most machines which process the data do not sense this corner cut, although some machines are designed to stop if the cut is not in the right position. Other visual aids include colored cards, striped cards, and edge stripes. These are all designed to simplify the problem of identifying different *decks* of cards or of determining from what deck a particular card came. In addition, anything may be written on the cards as a visual aid since the machines do not read the writing. Thus, it is common practice to mark the top card of a deck, "first card," and the bottom card, "last card," especially if the deck is to be used many times. A brief description of the contents of the deck is sometimes written on the first card.

The shape of the corner is unimportant to the machines which process the cards. The corners then may be rounded as shown in Fig. 5-2 or they may be square as in Fig. 5-1. Cards with rounded corners require an extra operation in manufacture and are consequently more expensive. However, if the card is to be used repeatedly, square corners tend to fray sooner than rounded ones.

The machines which process the cards cause wear, and a worn card can jam a machine. Occasionally a machine gets out of order and chews up a few cards before it is stopped. In many applications a deck of cards is used over and over many times. An example is a utility company which has a separate card for each customer. If cards were destroyed or too worn to work in the machines, the cards would have to be replaced. It is common practice to prepare a duplicate deck of cards immediately and store the master deck in a safe place. When cards are destroyed they can easily be duplicated from the master deck.

The storage conditions of the master deck are important, since paper has a tendency to become brittle and take on a curvature if not stored correctly. Cards should be stored standing on their edges rather than lying flat and should be kept under pressure. The storage drawers or boxes should be kept at a temperature between 60 and 80°F and a humidity between 20 and 40 percent. When it is necessary to duplicate a deck, the new deck can become the master, and the old master would then be put into use.

Before a deck of cards is inserted in a machine, the cards should be fanned slightly to get rid of static electricity. The cards are then aligned and put into the processing machine. Incidentally, it is common terminology to say the *cards* are processed. More exactly, the *data* on the cards are processed.

IBM cards may be perforated. Thus, the bill from a gasoline company is an IBM card which is divided into two sections. The customer tears the card on the perforations and retains one part for his own records. The punched part is returned with the check. The punched part is then processed on a machine specifically designed for it.

5-3 DISADVANTAGES OF PUNCHED CARD PROCESSING

The punched card is used in most business data-processing systems and yet it has many disadvantages. The cards may not be folded, spindled, stapled, or mutilated in any way. This is simply an annoyance that one learns to live with. The cards contain very little information in relation to their size. Thus only eighty symbols can be punched on a card, whereas it is possible to type about 2000 characters on a card of the same size. As was mentioned, the requirement that data be assigned to fields reduces the symbols per card to much less than eighty. There is, however, the advantage that these eighty symbols can represent more than eighty items of data, since any symbol can be a code for more information or a control punch instructing the machine to perform a specific function. Characters typed on a card, however, could also be used as codes indicating more information.

BIBLIOGRAPHY

GREGORY, R. H. and R. L. VAN HORN, *Automatic Data-Processing Systems.* Belmont, Calif.: Wadsworth Publishing Co., 1963. Chapter 2 discusses the layout of and coding of punched cards.

MOORE BUSINESS FORMS, INC., *Tab Cards.* This booklet describes the various types of IBM (i.e., tab) cards available to the user.

QUESTIONS

5–1
Herman Hollerith formed a company to develop data-processing equipment. This company later (after several mergers and name changes) became a leader in the data-processing field. What is the name of that company today?

5–2
What are some of the more common ways of referring to punched card data-processing machines?

5–3
What is the famous slogan of the IBM Corporation?

5–4
What are some of the more common ways of referring to punched card data-processing equipment as a separate and distinct class of data-processing equipment?

5–5
What is meant by the "unit-record" principle of data processing?

5–6
How many columns and rows are there on an IBM punched card?

5–7
What is meant by the term "field" in the sense in which it is used in data processing?

5–8
What is a *zone punch* and what is it used for?

5–9
What are the ways in which human beings (not the machines) can tell one punched card from another?

5–10
Do any of the things mentioned in Question 5–9 affect the machines' ability to recognize one card from another?

5–11
What does it mean to say, "twelve-edge first, face down"?

5–12
In what ways are the IBM and Sperry Rand cards different?

5–13
What zone punches are required for each of the following letters? K, F, W, L, and Z?

6

Machines for Processing Cards

6–1 INTRODUCTION

If punched card data processing is to compete with manual data processing, it must be competitive in accuracy, speed, and automation. In manual data processing, sales slips and other records are processed as they are. In punched card processing, however, the information from sales slips, time cards, invoices, and other records must first be entered on tab or punched cards in the form of punches or holes. This represents an extra operation and to make it worthwhile, a large number of machines have been designed to handle the cards (after they are manually punched) automatically and process the data faster than can be done manually.

In all data-processing systems, the information on sales slips, time cards, bills, etc., must first be translated to a medium that the machines can handle. Tab cards are one such medium. The documents which contained the original data are called *source documents*. The cards punched with information from the source documents are used as input to the machine. (Other types of input media, which special machines can handle, are punched-paper tape and magnetic tape.)

Manufacturers of data-processing machines have designated the machines by numbers as well as names. It is customary to speak of the machine by the number designation, as for example a 24 instead of a keypunch, since there are many keypunches on the market. In general, it is neither necessary nor desirable to try to remember all the numbers and associated names. The numbers of the machines one works with are usually learned without effort.

All card machines must have a place to insert decks of cards (whether blank or punched) and a place to stack the cards after they are processed. These are called the *hopper* and *stacker*, respectively. Cards are fed into

48

a hopper, either singly or in a deck. After processing, the cards are neatly stacked in a stacker for easy removal. A machine for a special application may have more than one hopper or stacker. The machines will be described according to function.

6–2 KEYPUNCH

The machine which puts the holes in the cards is called a *keypunch* or simply a *punch*. It is possible to punch a tab card using a hand punch which punches the appropriate holes when a lever is moved. This is a slow process, however, and would be used only where a small number of additional cards are needed. In general, cards are punched on automatic keypunches such as the IBM 24, which is shown in Fig. 6-1. Since most automatic keypunches have features similar to those in the 24, we will use it as an example.

The card hopper in the 24 is at the upper right of the machine and holds up to 500 cards. The cards are inserted face forward with the nine-edge down. This may vary in other machines, but instructions are usually attached at the hopper. At the touch of a button, cards are fed down to the *card bed* and move across it from right to left. As the card moves, it passes under a punching station and then—about a card's length away—under a reading station. When it reaches the left-hand end of the bed, it is lifted and placed in the stacker, and at the same time a new card is fed from the hopper to the right-hand end of the bed. At the end of the run, all the cards will be in the stacker in the same order in which they were placed in the hopper.

At the start, two cards are brought down from the hopper. As the first is punched at the punching station, the second remains in place. When punching of the first card is completed, the card moves to the reading station; the second card moves to the punching station, and a third card moves down to wait its turn. Now *two* cards will move simultaneously, one under the reading station and one under the punching station, until the deck is exhausted.

Punching is done by hitting the keys of a keyboard similar to that of a typewriter. As each key is

Fig. 6-1. IBM 24 Keypunch. (Courtesy of IBM.)

hit, the proper Hollerith code is punched in the column under the punching station, and the card is then advanced by one column. If the machine is to be used to punch only numerals, it is possible to buy one equipped with only a *numerical* keyboard. However, in most cases, letters and numbers are needed, so the full keyboard is required. A mixture of letters and numbers is referred to as *alphameric.*

It is possible to repeat all or part of the punches on several cards. For example, one field on the card may be used for the date and require the same holes on every card. In this case, the machine will duplicate the desired punches when a special button is pushed. To do this, the information is read from the card at the reading station and is duplicated on the next card at the punching station.

The operations described above are performed manually. That is each punch in the card is made by pushing a key for the desired alphameric character or by pushing the duplicate button so that the machine will punch a duplicate of the code on the card at the reading station. However, it is possible to automate a large part of the operation. Before describing how this is done, it is desirable to present a practical example where automatic punching is advantageous.

6–3 EXAMPLE

For our example, we will consider a department store where the information on individual sales slips is to be put on cards. The eighty columns of the card are divided into fields, perhaps as shown in Fig. 6-2. The first five columns may be left blank. Columns 6–10 are used for the sales slip number, so that in case of error, the card can be checked against the proper source document (sales slip). Columns 11–16 will contain the

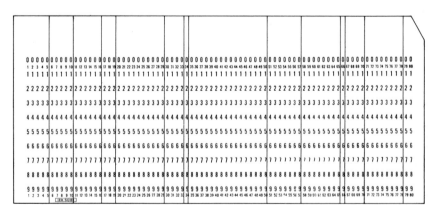

FIG. 6-2. Fields on IBM card.

date. Columns 17–19 are left blank. Columns 20–29 will contain the customer's account number. The first two digits of this number (columns 20 and 21) may be used to show the billing date. Columns 30–33 will show how many items of the article described in columns 35–50 are sold. Column 34 is blank. The single unit price goes in columns 51–57 and the total cost in 58–65. Column 66 is left blank. Columns 67–70 will be used for the salesman's number and 71–78 for his department. The last two columns can contain the card type, which is simply a number selected to show that the card represents a sales slip. Different numbers would be used on cards for payroll, accounts receivable, etc. All the information, except the card type, is contained on the sales slip.

To punch the information manually, the operator would first push the space bar five times since the first five columns are blank. He will now punch in the sales slip number. For our example, let us assume that all the sales slip numbers consist of two letters of the alphabet followed by three numerals. On the keyboard, the numerals occupy the same keys as some of the letters, and it is necessary to push a shift key to discriminate between letters and numerals. Thus, the operator pushes the alphabetic shift key for the first two digits of the number and then the numeric shift key for the last three. He punches the date in columns 11–16. Columns 17–19 are skipped. He punches the customer's account number in columns 20–29, making sure to use all the columns. In effect, the first two digits represent the day of the month on which a bill will be sent, starting with 01 for the first and ending with 30 for the thirtieth. The thirty-first is not normally used as a billing date. (If a billing date falls on a Sunday or holiday, bills are sent on the next working day.) Columns 30–50 contain the order, beginning with numbers for quantity, then a space, and then letters for description. The price per unit and total cost are punched in their appropriate fields. The rest is self-explanatory. Note that the fields are referred to by the term indicating their practical use. Thus columns 6–10 make up the *sales slip* field; 11–16 is the *date* field, etc.

It should be noted that the six columns for the date have to be filled completely. That is, the month of January must be represented as 01, for example, since a one in the first column might be confused with 10 for October. In a similar manner, ambiguities can occur in the quantity field, unless care is taken.

When this job is automated, the blank spaces are skipped automatically. Thus, the card moves right to column 6 to start and, after column 16 is punched, it moves to column 20. Likewise, after 33 is punched, it moves to column 35, and after 65 is punched, it moves right to 67. Also, anything which is the same for all cards is duplicated automatically. In this example, the date in columns 11–16 and the card type in columns 79–80 are duplicated automatically. In addition, any time the operator notices that the information to be entered in a field is the same as that on the preceding card, he can push a duplicate button once, and the whole field is duplicated. This might occur, for instance, if the same salesman was represented on two successive sales slips. The shifting from alphabetic characters to numerals and back is also automatic.

The skipping, duplicating, and alphabetic shifting are controlled by a *program* card. This is a tab card which is divided into the same fields as the cards being punched. The program card is punched with four *program codes*, twelve, eleven, zero, and one. Every column in each field, except the first column of the field, is punched in the twelve-row. The twelve-row punches are said to *define the field*. An eleven-punch indicates "start automatic skip," and a zero-punch means "start automatic duplication." The skip and duplicate punches occur in the first column of a field, and the action, once started, continues as long as there is a twelve-punch in the next column. Ordinarily when the machine is set to run automatically, it will punch a numeral when a key is pushed. To make it punch a letter, shifting is controlled on the program by a hole in the one-row.

A program card for the sales slips cards of our example is shown in Fig. 6-3. The eleven-hole in column 1 indicates automatic skip. Since twelve is punched in the next four columns, the machine skips over these and stops at column 6. The eleven-punch in column 34 also indicates "start skipping," but since there is no twelve-punch in column 35, only a single column is skipped. The one-punch in columns 6 and 7 shifts the keyboard to make it punch a letter of the alphabet. The one-punch also is shown in columns 35–50, where a description of the article sold is to be punched. The twelve-punches in columns 36–50 allow automatic

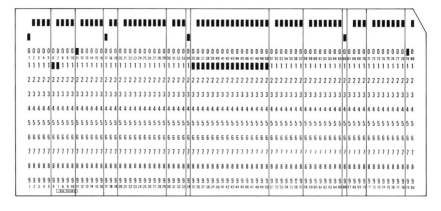

Fig. 6-3. Program card for keypunch.

skipping whenever the name of the article stops short of column 50. With-out these twelve-punches, an operator would have to depress the skip key manually for every column from the end of the name through column 50. All other punches are numeric. The zero-punch in column 11 indicates "start duplicating." The machine will duplicate column 11 and continue through 16 because the twelve-holes are punched there. Since there is no twelve-hole in column 17, the machine stops duplicating there. The eleven-punch in 17, followed by twelves in 18 and 19, causes these to be skipped, and the card moves right to column 20 where there is no twleve-punch. The zero-punch in column 79 and twelve-punch in column 80 cause these two columns to be duplicated from card to card. In operation, the date and card type would be entered manually on the first card along with the rest of the data. From then on these fields would be duplicated automatically, being punched at the punching station exactly the same as what is read at the reading station on the preceding card.

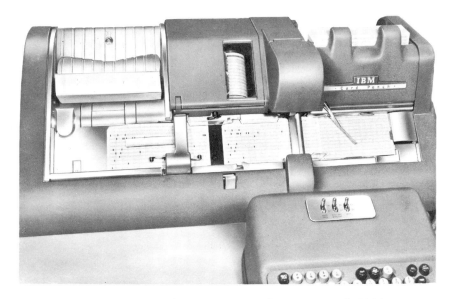

Fig. 6-4. Close-up of IBM 26 Keypunch. (Courtesy of IBM.)

Strictly speaking the twelve-holes punched on the program card in fields where manual punching will occur are unnecessary. However, they permit the operator to duplicate a field or skip a field by pressing the appropriate skip button only once on the keyboard. For example, if two successive sales slips are for the same article, the operator can duplicate the description field by pressing the duplicate button once at the start of this field.

If the operator catches an error, he can correct it at once without having to punch the whole card over manually. Suppose he makes an error in column 50. He simply pushes the release key which advances the card to the reading station, and a new card moves to the punching station. Now by pressing appropriate keys, he can duplicate the first 49 columns, which are correct, and then finish the card normally. The wrong card is removed immediately and destroyed.

The 26 is another IBM keypunch which can print on the card the character which is punched. The printing appears above the twelve-row with each character directly above the column in which it is punched. This is illustrated in Fig. 5-2. A keypunch which can print the characters in this fashion is called a *printing punch*.

The program card is easily removable so that the operator can insert the proper program card for the particular job to be done. On the 24 and 26, the program card is mounted on a drum at the top center of the machine. This drum rotates so that the column visible through a window at the front of the machine corresponds to the column on the card at the punching station. Figure 6-4 is a close-up of the 26, showing the program card on the drum.

6–4 VERIFIER

It is very important that cards be punched correctly or all subsequent processing will be in error. Thus, after cards are punched, but before they are used, they are usually checked for correctness. This can be done on a machine like the IBM 56 *Verifier*. This machine resembles the 24 or 26 keypunch; however, the punching station of the 24 is replaced by a verifying station on the 56.

The operator wishing to verify cards puts the deck in the hopper of the 56 and proceeds exactly as if he were punching on the 24. Now, when a key is pushed it must agree with the code already punched on the card at the verifying station. If the complete card agrees with what the operator "punches," a small notch is cut in the card on the right-hand edge between the zero- and one-rows. This is called the OK notch. If the operator pushes a key which does not agree with what is on the card, the keyboard locks and a red light goes on. The operator then must press the *error-release key*, which unlocks the keyboard, and then try the correct key again. If he made a mistake the first time and is correct on the second trial, the error light goes off and he proceeds to verify the rest of the card. A third trial is permitted, if the second still shows an error, but after the third trial, the keyboard unlocks and the card can be finished. However, if the error persists through the third trial, an *error notch* appears above the column in error and the OK notch is omitted.

6–5　SORTER

As its name implies, a sorter is a machine for sorting a deck of cards into smaller piles in alphabetic or numerical sequence. The IBM 83 Sorter, shown in Fig. 6-5, is capable of sorting 1000 cards per minute. The 83 has a hopper, in which the deck of cards is placed, and 13 stackers to receive the sorted cards. The sorter can operate on only one column at a time, but this column can be chosen by setting a selection lever manually. The machine senses from the nine-edge up toward the twelve, and as soon as a hole is detected, the card is dropped into the stacker or pocket corresponding to that row. If no hole is located in the chosen column, the card drops into the right-hand pocket, which is designated the *reject* pocket. It is possible to set the machine to ignore specified rows.

In sorting alphabetically it is necessary to run the deck through the machine twice, since there are two holes in each column. In the first sort, the cards will drop into the first nine pockets, labeled (from the left) 9, 8, 7, 6, 5, 4, 3, 2, 1. These are then put back in the hopper in this order, and the machine is set to ignore these nine punches. Now the sorter will sense the zone punches only and will drop the cards into the next three pockets, labeled 0, 11, and 12. The cards in the 12-pocket will contain all the cards from A to I, arranged alphabetically; the 11-pocket will hold J through R, and the 0-pocket will hold S through Z.

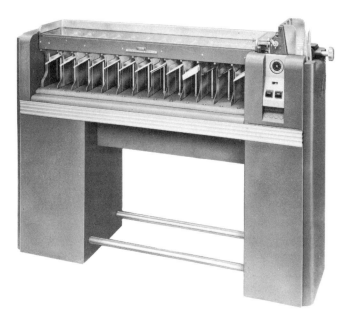

Fig. 6-5. IBM 83 Sorter. (Courtesy of IBM.)

If the sort is to cover more than one column, the right-hand column of the field is sorted first, and the sort progresses to the left. Similarly, if sorts are to cover more than one field, the less important field is covered first. In this case, the major division is called the *major sort,* and divisions within this sort are called the *minor sort.* For example, if cards are to be sorted by dates (month and day), the day field is sorted first as a minor sort, and then the month field becomes the major sort.

6–6 INTERPRETER

When cards are punched on a printing punch such as the 26, it is simple to read what is punched, since it is printed across the top of the card. However, if a keypunch like the 24 is used, this printed information is omitted. Also, in the course of processing cards, new cards are punched which, in general, do not contain the printed information. It is not difficult to figure out what is punched on a card, since the Hollerith code is easily learned. However, if it becomes necessary to check several cards, the work can be simplified by using a *card reader* or *interpreter.*

An interpreter is simply a machine which reads cards and prints on the face of a card exactly what is already punched there. The location of the printing varies with the interpreter but is usually near the top of the card. On the IBM 557 the printing can be made to occur in any of 25 lines across the face of the card. The hopper of the 557 holds 800 cards. These are fed and printed at the rate of 100 cards per minute. An optional feature of the machine is limited sorting into four stackers.

The printing in the interpreter does not occur over the column which is being interpreted. In the 557 and other IBM interpreters, the printing unit prints only 60 characters across the face of the card. To print 80 columns requires two lines of printing, and therefore two passes through the machine.

Another interesting feature of the 557 and other interpreters is the ability to print from one card onto another. A master card can be placed in the print unit, and information from it can be printed on all cards passing through the machine. This is not interpreting, but is a useful fringe benefit of having the printing unit.

An interpreter which reads cards and prints elsewhere is generally called a *card reader,* although the two terms are frequently used interchangeably. Figure 6-6 illustrates a card reader manufactured by Friden and designated ACR. The ACR holds 200 cards in its hopper at the top. These are fed through the machine, and the information on the cards is translated into electrical impulses to operate other Friden machines. In particular, the ACR can be connected to Friden's 2201 Flexowriter®,*

---

* Trademark held by Friden.

card passes the read station, the same field is punched on the next card, and so on. Since the same holes are punched on all cards (for this field), the punching can be verified by *sight checking*. This process consists of holding the aligned deck up to a source of light and observing that the punches go right through the deck.

Summary punching is automatic punching of totals used for accounting purposes. A reproducing punch like the 519 can be connected by cable to an accounting machine to operate as a summary punch. In this mode of operation, accounting totals printed at the accounting machine are automatically punched by the summary-punching circuits in the 519.

The 519 also has a printing unit for printing up to eight digits of information on the cards passing through it. The printing and reproducing can occur simultaneously. The information to be printed can be taken from the card itself, in which case the 519 acts as an interpreter, or it can be transcribed from a master card at the read station.

6-9 ACCOUNTING MACHINE

Data punched on cards can be manipulated by an *accounting machine*, which then prints out desired information. A typical punched card accounting machine is the IBM 407, illustrated in Fig. 6-7. The hopper and feeder are at the left, and a carriage and printing unit extend across the top. Information punched in cards can be processed at the rate of 150 cards per minute. The hopper holds about 1000 cards.

In its simplest mode of operation, the cards are read as they pass through the machine, and the information punched on the cards is printed

Fig. 6-7. IBM 407 Accounting Machine. (Courtesy of IBM.)

on a form (paper) in the carriage of the printing unit. This is called *listing*. In this mode, the machine is acting in the same manner as the combination of the Friden ACR and Flexowriter®, described in Section 6.6. In both the 407 and the Friden Flexowriter®, the printing can be controlled to appear wherever it is desired on the form. Both machines also can be controlled to print only portions of what is on the cards, a process called *selective printing*.

In the 407, amounts punched in cards can be added to or subtracted from amounts in other cards, and the new figures can be printed in proper places on the forms. This operation is called *accumulating*. It is also possible to combine two or more amounts punched on a single card, to keep track of several different groups of cards during a run, and to provide totals for each group.

As was explained in the description of the reproducing punch, the 407 can be connected to the 519 by cable. Then the 519 will produce summary-punched cards for the totals printed by the 407. If desired, the 407 will not print the information on each card, but will print only totals for a group of cards and perhaps a statement identifying the group. This is called *group printing* or *tabulating*.

6–10 CONTROL CIRCUITS

In all the card machines, it should be noted that each machine can perform more than one function. In addition, each job may require a slightly different kind of operation from the machine during its performance of a specific function. This was illustrated in the description of the program card for the keypunch. As long as sales slips are being processed, the program card of Fig. 6-3 can control the job. If, however, time-sheet data are to be punched, a new program card would be used, but the first one would be saved for use when sales slips are to be punched again.

The need for control is illustrated also in the description of the accounting machine. In the simple operation of listing, information from the punched cards is printed in the *proper* places on a form. The "proper" place is determined by

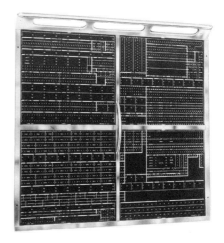

Fig. 6-8. Control panel of IBM 407. (Courtesy of IBM.)

6–7

How long would it take you to interpret (print) 5000 cards, using the IBM 557 Interpreter, if you wanted to print what was punched into 75 columns?

6–8

Write some examples of merging with card selection and matching with card selection, using the IBM 88 Collator as the basis for your examples.

6–9

On the IBM 519 Document Originating Machine is it possible to duplicate (or reproduce) a deck of cards and at the same time gang-punch data into the new cards? If it is possible, give an example of when you might want to do this.

6–10

What is the term used to describe the process of holding cards up to a light source to verify that certain punches appear in a complete deck of cards?

6–11

What is the purpose of having a *control panel* for data-processing machines?

7

Punched Cards In Business

7–1 APPLICATION OF PUNCHED CARDS IN BUSINESS

In the section on the keypunch in Chapter 6, we presented a rather detailed description of punching information from sales slips onto tab cards. We shall now trace the progress of the cards to illustrate how punched-card data processing is applicable in business. It is assumed that the cards have been punched as described, one card for each item on a sales slip, and that the punched cards can then be verified. If the cards were punched on a 24 keypunch, they would probably be verified on a 56. However, if a printing punch like the 26 is used, verification can be simply a visual comparison of the printing at the top of the card and the data on the sales slip. Once the cards have been properly punched, the sales slips can be stored in dead storage.

At this point, it may be cheaper to duplicate all the cards and have two identical decks than to make one deck serve many functions. One of the decks can then be used solely for billing and collecting, while the second deck is used for checking inventory, figuring commissions of salespeople, and analyzing effectiveness of individual departments or products. Therefore, the original deck would be run through a reproduction punch such as the 519, which can duplicate 1000 cards in ten minutes. Two decks would then be available.

One of the decks is now used only for accounts receivable. First it must be sorted. Since it will be used to prepare bills, a useful sort is by billing date (that is, by the first two digits of each customer's account number). Each day's deck of new cards is sorted on a machine like the 83. Two passes are necessary, first for column 21 and then for column 20. For 1000 cards, this takes about two minutes on the 83. The cards will then be sorted into 30 piles for the 30 billing dates. These are added to the *billing files* which contain 30 drawers or partitions. On a particular date, the cards in the drawer for that date are taken out to prepare the bills. For example, on the seventh day of the month, the cards in the drawer labeled 07 will be pulled out. All of these cards will have a zero punched in column 20 and a seven in column 21. While these cards are out being processed or awaiting payment, new cards may be added to drawer 07 as new purchases are made. These will be billed on the seventh of the next month. In the special case of February, the cards from drawer 29 are billed along with those in 28 and those in drawer 30 are billed on the first of March along with those in the drawer labeled 01.

It is necessary to have an index relating the customers' names and addresses with their account numbers. This would be arranged alphabetically by name, so that if a customer wanted information about his account and did not know his account number, it could be located. In order to simplify the card processing, this information should be punched on cards also. On the sales slip cards, the customer account number appeared in columns 20–29. These same columns should be used for the account number on the *customer cards*. (There is nothing special about columns 20–29; any columns could be chosen, but they should be the same on both kinds of cards.) The customer's name can be punched in columns 1–19 and his address in columns 30–78. The last two columns are again used to show the card type. For our example, let sales slip cards be designated 23 and customer cards 99. Thus, a two in column 79 and a three in column 80 indicate that the card represents a sales slip. Nines in both of these columns mean a customer card. The customer cards are also kept in a file of 30 drawers or compartments, arranged by billing dates. It is not necessary to arrange them numerically beyond this.

On the seventh of the month, for example, the operator removes the 99-cards from the 07 drawer of the *customer file* and the 23-cards from the 07 drawer of the *billing file*. The customer cards are placed under the sales slip cards, and the total pile is placed in a sorter such as the 83, to sort by customer account number. Since columns 20 and 21 are the same on all cards, eight sorts are necessary to sort the eight remaining columns of the account number. The 83 sorts at the rate of 1000 cards per minute, so eight sorts are quickly finished. At this point, the cards are arranged numerically by account number. (To check this, the cards may be run through a collator such as the 88.) There are groups of cards with the same number, since some customers made more than one purchase during the month. Each group of 23-cards is followed by a 99-card with the same account number. There are also some customers cards with no sales slip cards preceding them, since some customers made no purchases during the month. The new deck of cards is now put in a 407 accounting machine which is cabled to a machine that can do summary punching, such as the 519. As each sales slip card is fed through, the 23 in the last two columns is sensed, and the date of sale and total price are printed on a bill form in the carriage of the 407. When the last sales slip card in a group has been fed through the machine and a customer card is at the reader, the nine in column 80 is sensed. This "instructs" the machine to print in the column headed "balance due," a total of the items already entered. Also, the customer's name and address are printed on the form. The 519 punches a summary card, containing the customer's account number and total amount billed. This card is to be used to compare with the check which will be received from the customer. Alternatively, instead of using a 519, the 407 can print a carbon copy of the bill to be used when the check arrives.

As soon as one bill is finished, a new form is fed to the carriage of the 407 accounting machine and the process is repeated. If a customer had no purchases in the month, his customer card would follow another customer card instead of one or more sales slip cards. In this case, no bill should be prepared. This can be programmed into the control circuit. Note that in the process just described, the nine in column 80 caused the machine to print the total bill and the customer's name and address. The nine in column 79 can be used to "instruct" the machine to ignore following cards until a card with 23 in columns 79 and 80 is read. In this way bills are prepared only for customers who made purchases.

When the bills are finished, the customer cards must be separated from the others. This can be done by using a sorter, working on one column which differs in the two sets. Either column 79 or 80 will do. Also, any of the first five columns could be used, since they are blank on the sales slip cards. The customer cards are returned to the customer file. The duplicate bills or summary cards are placed in the accounts receivable file. The sales slip cards should be destroyed, since they have served their purpose, and the original source documents are available if any question arises.

When checks arrive, they can be compared with the copies of the bills in accounts receivable. If summary cards are used, they can be sorted to find the cards corresponding to the customers who sent checks. Some provision must be made to detect cards or copies which have been in the accounts receivable file for too long a time. They represent delinquent accounts. This can be done in a number of ways, which will be left to the imagination of the students.

The process of preparing bills, as described, may sound cumbersome and inefficient. Nevertheless, once the system is set up, it enables one operator to print all the bills in a much shorter time, with less effort, and more accuracy than can be done manually. The system can be improved. For example, when gasoline is purchased on credit, the customer immediately receives a *copy* of the sales slip. The sales slip is a card which is returned to the company's office. This card is shorter than an 80-column card, but is punched in the same code. That is, the sales slip itself is punched with the customer's account number and cost of the purchase. All the cards are fed into an electronic calculating punch, which adds all the cards for each customer and punches a summary card. An interpreter then prints the bill on the summary card. The bill is the size of a full IBM card but it is perforated between the 27th and 28th columns. The customer tears the card on the perforation, retaining the short left-hand part for his records, and returns the punched right-hand part with his check. This is then automatically compared with a duplicate summary card, and the customer's account is shown as paid.

Of course, the value of the check must cover the amount due. In practice, this will be true most of the time, but occasionally a customer will underpay or overpay. Then it is necessary to carry the balance. This can be punched on a card, if the accounts receivable file contains tab cards, or it can simply be typed on a bill form by using the 407 to compute the balance and do the printing.

The duplicate deck, which was prepared originally, can be used for many different purposes. For example, in many department stores, sales people are paid a salary plus a commission on sales. The duplicate deck can be used to determine quickly the total sales of each salesman. This would probably be done weekly. The cards would be sorted by salesmen's numbers, columns 67–70. Just as we had customer cards in the previous example, we must have *salesman cards* in this. These might be numbered 45 (in columns 79 and 80). The salesmen's numbers would be punched in columns 67–70, just as on the sales slip cards. The salesman cards can be interleaved with the sorted deck, using a collator like the 88, or they could be added to the deck before it is sorted, as was done with the customer card for the billing function. Now we can use the same procedure as above, but instead of getting bills, we get a total of sales for each salesman.

Note that the six manipulations of data occur when cards are used. In the billing example above, first the data must be *recorded*. This is done by punching the facts on a tab card. The cards must be *classified*. The sales slip cards were classified by punching 23 in the last two columns; the customer cards were identified by 99 in the same place. The cards must be *sorted*. The 23- and 99-cards were sorted by billing date, but the 45-cards were sorted by salesman's number in columns 67–70. *Calculating* was done on the 407 accounting machine, and *summarizing* was done by using this machine cabled to a 519. Finally, all the manipulations were steps in the *communicating* process. Instead of transmitting information orally or by writing on a piece of paper, it is punched on cards, and the cards are transmitted from place to place.

In the department store example, various operations affecting the processing of data occurred. When a purchase was made, a sales slip was prepared. This is *selling*. The sales slip and, later, the punched card are a record of the sale and are thus considered associated with selling. If the customer took his purchase with him, this was *delivery*. If not, the item would be delivered later. A notation would be made on the sales slip to this effect, and an extra punch would be entered on the tab card. This might be in columns 17–19 and might even indicate the day of delivery or the driver. As we saw, the operations of *billing* and *collecting* were aided by using the punched cards. The salesman cards were used to figure commissions, which would be paid. This is part of the *disbursing* operation. The whole payroll is, of course, disbursing.

Inventory is controlled by punched cards in many businesses. Let us consider an operation like Jim's Janitorial Service, described in Chapter 4, only much larger. With a large stockroom which has tools, cleaning supplies, light bulbs, and many other items, it would be difficult for one clerk to control and maintain inventory without some automation, and a punched card inventory system can be used to advantage. On the front of each bin in the stockroom is a pocket which holds a tab card. The card is punched with the name of the item in the bin, the number on hand, the reorder level, and the reorder amount. For example, let us suppose that we have 150 sponges in stock, and that we reorder 200 sponges whenever the number drops to 20 or less. Our *inventory card* might have the name in columns 10–20, the amount in columns 25–30, the *reorder level* in 35–40 and the *reorder amount* in columns 45–55. In this case the card for sponges would have the word *SPONGES* in columns 10–16, the amount *150* in columns 28–30 (or 000150 in columns 25–30), the reorder level *20* in columns 30 and 40, and the reorder amount *200* in columns 53–55. Note that the reorder level is determined realistically. The number 20 might be chosen because it takes two days for delivery, but less than 10 sponges are requisitioned from stock each day. The reorder level is chosen after consideration of the space available, the frequency of reordering, and the capital required.

A foreman requisitions three sponges from the stockroom. Using a keypunch, the stockboy punches the number of items required on a blank card in columns 25–30 (the same columns as the quantity on hand on the inventory card). In this case, since the quantity is a single digit, it goes in column 30. In some of the unused columns of the card (before 10 or after 55), he may punch in data to indicate who requested the order. These data are not necessary for inventory, but may be used for other purposes by the manager of the company. The stockboy now drops the punched card in the pocket with the *item card* (also called, *commodity card*) on the front of the bin of sponges and gives the foreman three sponges. Since most of the requisitions are made in the morning, the cards can be processed after lunch. This can be done on any machine or combination of machines which will do summary punching. A multipurpose machine, called an *accumulating reproducer,* is sometimes used. The cards in each bin are placed in the hopper with the item card last. The machine takes a total of the amounts on the order cards and subtracts this from the amount on the item card. Two summary cards are prepared. One shows a total of the quantities ordered, as well as the name of the item. It may also have the date. This will be used for other purposes. The second is a new inventory card. Thus, if during the day, three people order a total of 10 sponges, there would be three amount cards (totaling 10). The new inventory card for sponges would have 140 in columns 28–30 instead of 150, but would be otherwise identical to the old card. If the reproducer does not print, the new inventory cards can be run through an interpreter, so that the stockboy can read the cards easily and put them back in the proper pockets.

Before the new inventory cards are returned to their proper pockets, they are checked for reordering information. Whenever the number in the amount field is less than that in the reorder field, the item must be reordered. This can be done on an accounting machine. The machine compares the two numbers, and if the item must be reordered, it prints out the quantity to be reordered (from columns 45–55) and the item name. If the amount on hand exceeds the reorder number, the card is fed through without printing. The result is a printed reorder list of all items in short supply. When the items arrive, a new inventory card is made in the same manner as the old, except the summary punch is programmed to add rather than subtract.

In this example, cards were used to control *inventory.* If items were bought when inventory was low, this was *purchasing.* When the order arrived, this was *receiving.* And, of course, *disbursement* took place when the items were paid for. In some situations, a low inventory is a signal to manufacture rather than purchase. This is *production.* In Jim's Janitorial Service, the delivery and production operations occurred simultaneously.

Each business has its own special accounting requirements. The data processing can usually be handled by punched cards, and there may be several different approaches, all of which work. Cost and time are the deciding factors. It would be a waste of money to design a system which requires, for example, a 519 reproducer, but uses the 519 only ten minutes a week. In a well designed system, maximum use is made of every machine in the system. Although the design of the data-processing system is an advanced subject, the student can benefit by trying to imagine how different machines can be used in various business operations. There is really no wrong answer, of course, but some systems are more ingenious and imaginative than others.

BIBLIOGRAPHY

CANNING, R. G., *Electronic Data Processing for Business and Industry.* New York: John Wiley and Sons, Inc., 1956. This book is a classic and discusses electronic data processing as a management tool. Also covered are equipment characteristics, computer programming, and systems design.

DIEBOLD, JOHN D., *Automation.* Princeton, N. J.: Van Nostrand Co. Inc., 152. This text presents an early presentation of the implications of the feedback concept and its applications.

GOLDRING, M. S., "Electronics and the Banks," *The Banker,* March, April, May, 1953. The application and impact of the early data processing equipment on banks is given.

LESSING, LAWRENCE P., "Computers in Business," *Scientific American,* Jan. 1954, pp. 21–25. The history and early application of computers to some business problems are discussed in this article.

THE NATIONAL CASH REGISTER CO., *What is a Computer? NCR Electronic Data Processing Written for the Layman,* Book 3, SP-1553-C-A 7RRR. This is a good introductory pamphlet describing what a computer is and how one would use tab cards with the computer. It is well written and easily understood.

The student should read "Computers in Business," *What is a Computer?,* and one of the other three.

QUESTIONS

7–1
What is the advantage of using the 519 Document Originating Machine in the case problem discussed in Chapter 7?

7–2
Why is it so very important to verify the punching in the cards created from the source documents?

7–3
What are the advantages of making a duplicate deck of billing cards as used in the case problem in Chapter 7?

7–4
Which of the nine basic business operations are represented by the billing being done on the IBM 407 Accounting Machine and the summary punching being done on the 519 Document Originating Machine?

7–5
What are some other examples of the nine basic business operations that might be more efficiently handled by means of business data-processing equipment?

7–6

What is meant by *reorder level?*

7–7

Discuss the statement, "There is a right way and a wrong way of handling the data processing requirements of a business."

7–8

Can you think of some disadvantages of using business data-processing equipment in an organization?

7–9

Why would a business split up its customers into groups to be billed on different dates?

7–10

Why wouldn't it be a good idea for a small business, which could not afford data-processing equipment, to have its billing job done by some other company which could afford data-processing equipment?

PART 3

Computer Data Processing

8

Parts of a Computer

8–1 COMPUTER COMPONENTS

There is a tendency on the part of the public to try to "personalize" the electronic computer and to identify the parts of a computer as though they were parts of a human body. Thus people use the terms *brain* for the part of the computer which calculates, *nervous system* for the part which controls the operation of the computer, and *memory* for the part where information is stored. Although these terms do describe the functions of the various components, they also tend to make the computer appear more complicated than it really is. Unfortunately, the manufacturers also use the popular terms, thus compounding the confusion.

The basic difference between a computer and an ordinary desk calculator is the large storage capacity of the computer. The *storage unit*, or simply *storage*, is frequently termed *memory*, but it should be emphasized that it is not a memory unit in the human sense. When a manufacturer speaks of a two-megabit memory, he means a unit in which it is possible to *store* two million *bits* of information and from which it is possible to reclaim any desired bit or bits at will. [The prefixes mega (million) and kilo (thousand), are frequently used in describing storage units. A bit is the smallest possible unit of information. It will be described more fully later in this chapter.]

The storage unit can store digits, letters, and special characters, which can be *called* out of storage as needed. In fact, numbers can be called from storage and manipulated as required by the task at hand. The *results* of the arithmetic manipulations can then be returned to storage to be available when needed, either for more manipulations or for final printout.

Perhaps, the most distinctive characteristic of a computer is the fact that the *program* for the calculations to be performed is also stored in its storage unit, along with the numbers with which these calculations are to be

75

performed. A program is nothing more than a series of instructions which cause the computer to perform the desired operations in the desired order. It is important to note that, just as the computer can be instructed to manipulate numbers, it can also be instructed to select alternative paths of instructions. For example, in payroll calculations in 1965, social security deductions were made on gross income until $174 were deducted from an employee's pay (at the rate of $3\frac{5}{8}$ percent of gross income). The instructions stored in memory (or storage) may require the computer to calculate $3\frac{5}{8}$ percent of the amount of an employee's weekly earnings and then to search in the storage unit for the employee's total earnings and deductions to date. If the total social security deduction, including the new figure, is less than $174, the new figure is deducted from earnings. If the total exceeds $174, a new instruction is selected from storage, telling the computer to deduct only enough to make the total exactly $174.

The arithmetic manipulations are performed in the *arithmetic unit* of the computer. Numbers are taken from storage and manipulated according to instructions. Since many problems involve more than one manipulation, the arithmetic unit usually contains provision for a limited amount of temporary storage of results until they are called out of the machine. In addition, the arithmetic unit possesses the capability of making *logical* decisions, such as noting which of two numbers is larger. In our tax-deduction example above, the fact that no further deductions are made after the total reaches $174 is a logical decision, which is made by the arithmetic unit. Because of the logic capability, this unit is sometimes called the arithmetic-logic unit. The circuits in the arithmetic unit are either for manipulating or for storing. The manipulating circuits are usually called *adders*, since all the arithmetic functions are performed by adding. The storage part of the arithmetic unit is called the *accumulator*. In some computers there is no accumulator, but intermediate and final results are stored in the storage unit.

The part of the computer which controls the operations of all the components is called the *control* unit. This unit enables the computer to solve long complicated problems or process multitudes of data *automatically*. During a typical processing run, numbers are called from storage and manipulated. The results are stored temporarily in an accumulator until they are needed for more manipulations or are printed out. Everything must be done in a prescribed order. The control unit directs the flow of information and operation, so that messages going in opposite directions do not collide on the same wire and all operations are done in the order specified. For example, it allows adders to add two numbers only after the two numbers have arrived there from storage. Without this control, it is conceivable that an adder might start adding when only part of a number has reached it.

The control unit is housed in a *console,* a desklike structure, which acts as an external control center of the computer. The console has a series of lights, buttons, switches, and usually a typewriter keyboard which enables the operator to monitor the various circuits in the *processor.* The term "processor" (sometimes called *central processor*) is used to designate the combination of control unit, arithmetic-logic unit, and storage unit.

The computer must be fed information or data to be processed. The unit which receives the data is called the *input* or *input unit.* The final results after processing must come out of the computer. The unit which furnishes these results is called the *output* or *output unit.* Using the human analogy, the operator "talks" to the computer through its input, and the computer "answers" or talks to the operator through its output. Sometimes the input and output are contained in a single physical piece of equipment, which is then called an *input-output unit.*

Thus, the five parts of a computer are (1) its storage or memory unit, (2) its arithmetic or arithmetic-logic unit, (3) its control unit, (4) its input unit, and (5) its output unit. The first three are referred to as the central processor of the computer. We shall now consider these components in more detail.

8–2 STORAGE

A storage unit must be capable of receiving large quantities of information which it will then hold ready for almost instantaneous retrieval. When information is "moved" from storage to the arithmetic unit, it is not destroyed in the storage unit; that is, the information is not actually removed from storage. Instead, the arithmetic unit "looks at" the storage file and "sees" the information which it then uses in its computations. A *bit* is the smallest unit of information. Thus a hole in a punched card or a magnetized dot on magnetic tape may represent a bit, since it represents a unit of information. The absence of a hole may also represent a bit in some situations. This is analogous to asking a question which can be answered "Yes" or "No." The presence of the hole indicates an affirmative answer, but the absence of the hole, where an answer is expected, is just as informative, although negative. In business data processing, as opposed to scientific computing, the term *bit* is rarely used. Instead, the capacity of a storage unit is usually given in terms of characters, and it is understood that a group of bits is used to represent a number, letter, or other symbol according to a fixed *code. Coding* will be discussed in the next chapter.

One form of storage unit uses magnetic tape similar to that used in a home tape recorder. However, instead of storing words or music, the recording consists entirely of a series of magnetized dots, each group of dots representing a character. Magnetic tape may have more than 500 characters per inch recorded on its surface. Special high-speed tapes and high-speed recorders are used, so that the tape travels at a rate of 100 inches per second. The reading unit and writing unit are contained in a single device called the *read/write head*. As many as 25,000 characters pass this head per second and can be read out as needed.

In a tape-storage unit, several tapes are arranged in a bin, each tape formed in an endless loop. The read/write head can be directed to read a selected portion of a selected tape. In a typical storage unit of this type there may be as many as 50 individual loops of tape, each about 250 feet long. The total storage capacity is in excess of two million symbols. In some tape-storage units, the tape is on reels, as in a home tape recorder, instead of being in continuous loops. The reels wind and unwind at high speed during operation. In the continuous-loop units, the tape moves in the same direction all the time.

A widely used type of storage unit is the *magnetic core memory*. The core is simply an iron ring about fifty-thousandths of an inch in diameter which can be magnetized in either a clockwise or counterclockwise direction. By convention, magnetism in a clockwise direction represents a bit or a one, in the opposite direction, a zero. The same sort of code that is used on magnetic tape can be used to make symbols out of bits, but a separate core is needed for each bit.

A magnetic core memory is shown in Fig. 8-1. The individual cores are threaded at the intersections of a network of wires. Currents passing through the wires "write" into storage by magnetizing the cores. Reading is also done by sampling currents, but these currents remove the bit by magnetizing the cores in the opposite direction. It is then necessary to regenerate the bit by putting a second current through the core. In practice, this requires very little additional computer circuitry.

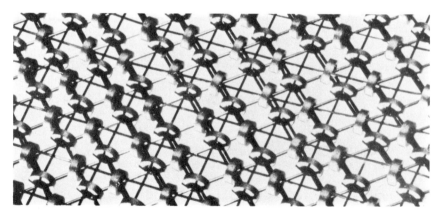

Fig. 8-1. Magnetic core memory. (Courtesy of IBM.)

FIG. 8-2. Friden 6018 Disk file. (Court

The *magnetic disk file* is another type of st
looks something like a phonograph record. Infor
sides of a disk by magnetized dots arranged in al
each side. In a *disk file* or *disk file storage*, as ma
on a vertical shaft and spun at about 60 rev
read/write head must select the proper disk an
disk and must then find the proper track. The
moves up and down along the spinning disks and
the disks at the proper place. In order to speed *ac*
the desired bit or bits, some disk files have severa
Figure 8-2 shows a typical disk file, the Friden (
can store 960 *words* of 64 characters each or a t
characters. A computer *word* is a related group o
single unit of information.

Magnetic drums are also used for storage. A m
cylinder with a magnetic surface coating. Informa
it in a series of tracks. In effect, each track is a s
A separate read/write head is used for each tr

mbers. As we shall see in the next chapter,
n our usual decimal notation when they are
r. However, we shall use decimal notation to
erform multiplication and subtraction.
iplication can be accomplished by successive
e wished to multiply 23 by 176. We could
ty-three times. A simpler and quicker method
6 to itself three times and then shift it to the
ice. Thus:

$$
\begin{array}{r}
\left.\begin{array}{r}
176 \\
176 \\
176
\end{array}\right\} \text{ 3 times 176} \\
\end{array}
$$

$$
\text{es 176} \left\{\begin{array}{r}
176 \\
176 \\
\hline
4048
\end{array}\right.
$$

we make use of the *nines-complement* and the
es-complement is what we get when we subtract

each digit of a number from nine. Thus, the nines-complement of 2567 is 7432. To subtract one number from another, we first take the nines-complement of the *subtrahend*. (The subtrahend is the number which is to be subtracted, and the number from which it is subtracted is called the *minuend*.) The nines-complement is *added* to the minuend. The final digit *one*, which is carried, is not placed in the answer but instead is added to the units column. This is an *end-around-carry*. For example, to subtract 2567 from 9504, we add the complement of 2567 as follows:

$$
\begin{array}{r}
9504 \\
+7432 \\
\hline
(1)\ 6936 \\
\end{array}
$$
$$
\rightarrow 1
$$
$$
\begin{array}{r}
\hline
6937
\end{array}
$$

Note that instead of subtracting 2567, we add 7432, which is the nines-complement. The left-hand digit one, in the answer, is carried back to be added to the units column.

When one subtracts by adding the nines-complement, it is necessary that the complement of the subtrahend have the same number of digits as the minuend. This means that if the original subtrahend has fewer digits than the minuend, we assume that it is preceded by enough zeros so that both have the same number of digits. Thus, to perform the subtraction 3527 − 48, we assume that the subtrahend is 0048 and its complement is 9951. Then,

$$
\begin{array}{r}
3527 \\
+9951 \\
\hline
(1)\ 3478 \\
\end{array}
$$
$$
\rightarrow 1
$$
$$
\begin{array}{r}
\hline
3479
\end{array}
$$

Division is done by multiple subtractions just as multiplication is done by multiple additions.

When we add two numbers, such as 3592 and 4339, we frequently have to carry numbers from one column to the next on the left. Thus in this example,

$$
\begin{array}{r}
3592 \\
4339 \\
\hline
7931
\end{array}
$$

we begin at the right. We say, $2 + 9 = 11$. Put down 1 and carry 1.

$1 + 9 + 3 = 13$. Put down 3 and carry 1. $1 + 5 + 3 = 9$. Put down 9. $3 + 4 = 7$. Put down 7. We might save the "carries" until later. Thus:

$$
\begin{array}{cc}
 & 3592 \\
 & 4339 \\
\hline
S & 7821 \\
\hline
C & 11 \\
\end{array}
$$

The S-row shows the sum of each column without regard to anything which is to be carried. The C-row shows the amount to be carried. If we now shift the C-column one space to the left and add, we have

$$
\begin{array}{c}
7821 \\
11 \\
\hline
7931 \\
\end{array}
$$

which is the same result we obtained in the first place. (The reader should check the foregoing arithmetical examples, using a pencil and paper until he is sure he understands the concept of using addition to subtract and to multiply.)

The adder circuits in the computer work in this fashion. The circuit which yields only the S-row is called a *half-adder*. With additional circuitry to shift the C-row to the left and add it to the S-row, we have a *full adder*.

During manipulations the numbers are taken from storage and placed in the accumulator. The answers also appear in the accumulator. Thus, it seems that computations are performed there, but in reality they are done in the adder as was described above.

The arithmetical manipulations and some other operations of the computer can be done serially or in parallel. In *serial* operation, each manipulation is performed separately, before another is begun. Thus, in our example above, $3592 + 4339$, first 2 is added to 9, then 9 to 3, then 5 to 3, then 3 to 4; the carry row is shifted; the right-hand carry is added to 2 in the sum, and then the left-hand carry is added to 8. In *parallel* operation, the first four steps are done simultaneously by four adders. As might be expected, parallel machines are much faster than serial machines but are also more expensive, since they require many more components.

8–4 CONTROL

Although it is at times difficult to identify the control unit of a computer as a separate entity, without it the computer could not operate. An important part of the control unit is the timing circuit, which is sometimes compared to the human heart. Timing circuits generate short pulses which are sent to all parts of the computer to keep all operations on schedule. Pulse times may be in fractions of a microsecond. During each pulse, information is moved, switches are opened or closed or manipulations are started. In this way, information is processed in set order, and intermediate results are moved to the proper locations to be combined with other intermediate results which are already there.

The control unit contains circuits in which instructions are stored while they are being interpreted and carried out. These circuits are called *instruction registers*. The part of the circuit which interprets the instruction and generates the signals to carry out the instructions is called the *decoder*. The operation, then, starts with an instruction moving from the storage unit to an instruction register, where a decoder interprets it and sends out signals to execute the orders.

8–5 INPUT

Punched cards or tab cards provide a very convenient method of feeding information into the data-processing system. Cards are inexpensive and can be easily stored. Even with computers which have no provision for card input, it is customary to punch the raw data on cards first and then use the cards to convert the information to a medium that the computer will accept. The part of a computer which handles tab cards is called a *read-punch* machine, which is a combination of a card reader and a card punch. Sometimes the reader and punch are two separate instruments. The many existing machines for handling cards (see Chapters 5, 6, and 7) can be incorporated in the data-processing system which uses a computer with card input.

Paper tape is similar to punched cards in that the characters are represented by holes punched into it. The tape is one inch or less wide, and each character is represented by combinations of holes across its width. The possible positions for the holes are called *channels*, and a *code* may require 5, 6, 7, or 8 channels. The code simply represents characters by position of holes on the tape, just as the Hollerith code on punched cards translates characters into holes on the card. Paper tape is read by light shining through the holes on photoelectric cells.

Both punched cards and paper tape are relatively slow methods of input. The fastest paper-tape readers can read about 100,000 characters per minute, and the fastest card readers about 3000 cards per minute. If each card is punched in all 80 columns, these card readers can thus read 240,000 characters per minute. A much faster method of supplying input to the machine uses magnetic tape similar to that used in home recorders. The fastest magnetic tape reader can read more than 10,000,000 characters per second. The information is coded onto the tape in the form of magnetic dots, which can be arranged in the same sort of code used on paper tape. In fast tape drives, the tape moves at speeds in excess of 100 miles per hour.

The information is placed on the tape when it passes a recording head, and everything previously recorded is erased. Thus, care must be taken to ensure that wanted records are not accidentally erased. Special reels having a *file protection groove* in the hub are used for permanent data. The groove disconnects the recording head on the recorder so that only the read head can operate.

In general, the input device is the slowest part of the computer. Calculations and manipulations are done in small fractions of seconds, much faster than the time required to get the information into the working storage unit of the computer. If the computer is slowed down because it must wait for all the information to be fed into it, it is said to be *input-limited* or *input-bound*. To enable the computer to work at full capacity, a separate storage unit called a *buffer* is used to accept the information from the input device. Thus, information is fed from the input device to the buffer storage at the same time that the computer is working on something else. The buffer may be a small part of the main storage reserved for the purpose or it may be a separate unit. When the computer is ready for the new data, the information in the buffer is transferred to the main storage so that the buffer is then available for new data. The transfer is performed almost instantaneously.

There have been many experimental attempts to make input devices which can read characters directly and some of these have been used successfully. The best-known is *Magnetic Ink Character Recognition* or MICR, which is used by banks. The digits from zero to nine are written in a distinctive type (called E 13B Font) with ink containing metallic powder. When the characters are to be read, the printing is first passed through a strong magnetic field which magnetizes the metallic powder and then through a reader which senses the magnetized areas. The small digits at the bottom of most checks are written in "magnetic ink," and can be read and sorted by magnetic ink readers at rates up to 20 checks per second.

Optical character recognition is still in its infancy, but optical readers are used in some areas, notably to read account numbers printed from gasoline credit cards. To avoid confusing the optical reader or *scanner*, the printing must be in a special type. Some scanners have read up to 1000 words per minute.

As was mentioned earlier, a typewriter is mounted on the control console. This is not usually considered an input device because it is a very slow method of getting information into the machine. However, it enables the operator to *type* changes into a program or to add data to be stored.

8–6 OUTPUT

As has been pointed out, many devices are used both for input and output. Thus, a card reader is used for input and a card punch for output, but frequently they are combined into one unit called a read-punch machine. This then is an input-output unit. The output, of course, would be punched cards which can be used for later processing. For example, it may be necessary to update a deck of cards showing inventory. The inventory deck can be put into the computer along with cards punched to indicate sales and purchases, and the output would be a new deck showing the latest inventory.

Similarly, in a system using paper-tape input, it may be desirable to have paper-tape output for further processing. Usually, paper-tape machines can both read and punch and are, therefore, input-output units. Magnetic-tape units and magnetic disks, also, are usually input-output devices.

The typewriter on the control console is not usually used for output, just as its use for input is also limited. However, the operator can type a question and receive an answer on the same platen. For example, after information on accounts receivable has been fed into storage, one may wish to know the answer to a specific question. Typically, the operator can ask (by typing), "What purchases were made by Mrs. Smith?" The access mechanism will then scan Mrs. Smith's account in memory, and the answer will be typed automatically. The operator can even ask, "Did anyone buy a mink coat?" To get this answer, the memory will be scanned completely, and the answer typed automatically.

For most applications, the form of output required is printed information. High-speed printers have been developed to print out the required data as fast as they are processed. These devices print by electronics on electrosensitive paper and require no mechanical movement. More common, however, are printers using type which prints on ordinary paper. These devices print paychecks, bills, and other forms used in the operation of a business.

The high-speed, electronic printer can be connected directly with the computer since its operation can keep up with the latter. The result is called *on-line* printing. When using a slower printer, the computer would be slowed down if it had to wait for the printing. The computer is then said to be *output-limited* or *output-bound*. Just as buffers are used on the input side, there is a buffer output in which the output data are recorded on magnetic tape, and later read and printed. This is called *off-line* printing.

Cathode-ray tubes are another form of output. The output data appear as printing on the face of the tube.

8–7   THE COMPUTER SYSTEM

The five parts of the computer may be housed in one or more cabinets to form a complete *data-processing* or *computer system.* The manufacturer of an electronic data-processing system offers a basic central processor to which a variety of input-output units and additional storage units can be added. Since the I-O (input-output) units are usually housed separately, they are frequently called *peripheral equipment.*

In order to present a clearer understanding of a system, we will discuss in some detail a typical data-processing system, the IBM 1440. This is a medium-size, high-speed business data-processing computer system. The basic components of the system include a processor with core storage, a card read-punch unit, a printer, auxiliary disk drive, and a console. Additional storage units, as well as other input-output equipment, are usually added. Different models of the same piece of equipment have different capacities, so that a customer can purchase or lease only the *amount* of computer capacity he needs. However, the units are flexible so that additional capacity can be purchased or leased later, as processing requirements expand.

The processing unit of the 1440 is designated 1441. It has a magnetic core storage, which varies from 2000 to 16,000 *storage positions,* depending on the model number. Each storage position consists of seven cores, of which six are used to represent an alphameric character and the seventh is used to check for error. There is no accumulator in the arithmetic part of the 1441, so that the results are stored in the same storage unit. This is called *add-to-storage.* Operations are performed serially, that is, one digit at a time.

The 1440 system includes the 1442 card read-punch, which comes in three models. Model 1 reads 300 cards a minute and punches 80 columns a second; Model 2 reads 400 cards a minute and punches 160 columns a second; and Model 4 is simply a card reader which can read 400 cards a minute. The first two read data from cards and punch summary information on the same cards after processing. If it is desirable to separate the read function from the punch function, a 1444 card punch or a second 1442 may be added on-line. The 1444 punches 250 cards a minute, but cannot read the cards.

The 1443 Printer is used in the 1440 system. This unit comes in various models which can print up to 600 lines a minute. Paper, on a continuous roll, is automatically fed into the machine, which may print a line of up to 144 characters.

The console of the 1440 is designated 1447 and also comes in several models. It is available with and without a typewriter and with various assortments of switches and displays. The displays tell the operator what is contained in core storage.

In practice, the working storag
of the 1440 is the magnetic con
memory in the 1441 processor.
separate unit is added for file sto
age. The recommended file storag
is the 1311 disk storage drive wit
a 1316 disk pack, shown in Fig. 8-8
The 1316 is simply a stack of si
magnetic disks with 10 recording
surfaces. (The two outside surface
are not used.) Each disk surface i
divided into 2000 sectors of 10
characters each, so that the six disk
can store up to 2,000,000 alpha
meric characters. The 1311 driv
rotates the stack at 1500 revolu
tions per minute and has a separat
read/write head for each surface
The 10 heads move in and ou
between the disks in a comb-like
arrangement. Thus, it is called a

Fig. 8-8. IBM Disk file. (Courtesy of IBM.)

comb-type access. At any one position of the heads, 20 sectors pass each
read mechanism in each revolution so that it is possible to read a total
of 200 sectors without any motion of the heads. The sectors on the disks
all bear individual addresses, and the heads can be directed to what is
entered at specific addresses. This is called *random access.* In some
applications, information is recorded on the disks (or other storage)
sequentially without addressing and is then read out sequentially. This
is called *sequential access.* The average *access time* is a quarter of a
second. This is the time required to find the desired sector and read out
the information on it. As many as five 1311 units may be connected
directly with the other units in the 1440 system for an on-line storage
capacity of ten million characters. In addition, any number of 1316 disk
packs may be kept in reserve separately, each with the file storage of a
different job. These weigh only ten pounds each and can easily be inserted in the 1311 as required.

The operation of the 1440 in a payroll situation is a good example of
data processing in action. Tab cards are punched on a keyboard, such
as the 26, to indicate hours worked. A separate card is used for each
employee. The cards are placed in the hopper of the 1442 read unit.
The cards are read, and the information is fed into the core memory of
the 1441 processor. The 1311 disk storage drive contains a 1316 disk
pack with payroll information. As each card's information arrives at the

oyee's number on the 1316. Here
ate, and various deductions. The
and deductions. These amounts
the new totals are placed in the
the old ones on the disks. (Just
g automatically erases what had
r prints the pay check on a con-

magnetic tape unit for file storage,
th the disk storage unit. The 7335
the rate of 20,000 characters a
on one inch of tape. Other equip-
1440 system includes paper-tape
magnetic ink character readers

BIBLIOGRAPHY

ENGINEERING RESEARCH ASSOCIATES, *High Speed Computing Devices*. New York: McGraw-Hill Book Co. 1950. This middle-level engineering text describes digital computers from the design viewpoint. This book, however, is somewhat dated.

SIEGEL, PAUL, *Understanding Digital Computers*. New York: John Wiley and Sons, Inc. 1961. This middle-level book describes logic and computer arithmetic, the various building blocks used in the construction of computers, and how the various parts of a computer work.

Either of these books can be read for additional information on the computer components.

QUESTIONS

8–1

What are the two major differences between a desk calculator and a computer?

8–2

What is meant by the statement that a computer can make logical decisions?

8–3

What is the purpose of having a control unit or control component in a computer system?

8–4

What happens in the *storage unit* of a computer system when some data are moved from one place in storage to another place in storage?

8–5

Would it be faster to retrieve data from a magnetic core storage unit or from a magnetic tape unit?

8–6

How is multiplication done in an electronic computer?

8–7

What is the sequence of events that takes place as the computer carries out one single instruction or command?

8–8

What are some of the more common input devices used in a computer system?

8–9

What are some of the more common output devices used in a computer system?

8–10

What is the only advantage of using a magnetic disk as auxiliary storage instead of using a magnetic tape unit?

9

Codes

9-1 DECIMAL AND BINARY SYSTEMS

In ordinary electromechanical, desk-type calculators, arithmetical manipulations are performed using our common decimal system. For example, a ten-toothed wheel may be used, with each tooth representing a digit from 0 to 9. The first large-scale computers were also electromechanical, but it was recognized that in order to increase speed and accuracy something better than the geared wheel was required. The geared wheel is a *ten-state* device; that is, it can be stopped in any of ten positions. This means that to reach a required position from an existing position, it might have to pass through five positions to get there. A *two-state* device would obviously be faster, since it moves from one position to only one other position. A two-state device also is less subject to error since it is either *on* or *off*, whereas in the ten-state device each digit is restricted to one-tenth of a revolution.

The early computers used relays or electromechanical switches which were either open or closed. In the open position, no current flowed; when closed, current flowed. The open position then represented "zero" and the closed position represented "one." The relay was a two-state device and was said to be *bistable*, which means it was stable in two positions. The electronic tubes and transistors which replaced the relays were also two-state devices in that they either passed or did not pass current, depending on control voltages. Special bistable circuits using transistors are now used. These are called flipflops since a voltage pulse of extremely short duration can flip them from one stable state to the other. The cores in a magnetic core storage unit are also two-state devices since they can be magnetized in either a clockwise or a counterclockwise direction. Strictly speaking they have three states, the third being *no* magnetism. However, once a core has been magnetized, it is

90

difficult to bring it to a state of no magnetic field whatsoever. In practice, magnetizing currents are large enough to swing the core from one magnetic state to the other, so the cores are used as bistable elements.

Since it was desirable to use bistable elements in the computer because of increased speed and accuracy, it became necessary to devise a method of expressing each number in our decimal system in some arrangement of zeros and ones. It should be noted that we are accustomed to count using the decimal system, probably because man has ten fingers. However, this is not the only system of counting. Thus, the decimal system has ten digits (*deci* is a prefix meaning "ten"); the *binary* system has two digits (the prefix *bi* means "two"); and there are other systems such as the *trinary* and *octal* systems. The binary system, using only two digits (zero and one), is ideally suited for the computer with bistable elements.

In the decimal system, we count from zero to nine, and then the next number is formed by a one followed by a zero. Using the same sort of rules, we can see that in the binary system, the order of numbers is 0, 1, 10, 11, 100, 101, 110, 111, 1000, etc. That is, a table of decimal and binary equivalents looks like this:

Decimal	Binary	Decimal	Binary
0	0	10	1010
1	1	11	1011
2	10	12	1100
3	11	13	1101
4	100	14	1110
5	101	15	1111
6	110	16	10000
7	111	17	10001
8	1000	18	10010
9	1001		

In the decimal system, any digit in a number represents the quantity of a certain power of ten. That is, for example, the number 3452 means

$$(2 \times 1) + (5 \times 10) + (4 \times 100) + (3 \times 1000)$$

or

$$(2 \times 10^0) + (5 \times 10^1) + (4 \times 10^2) + (3 \times 10^3).$$

In the same manner, a number in the binary system represents powers of two. For example, the binary number 1101 means

$$(1 \times 1) + (0 \times 2) + (1 \times 4) + (1 \times 8)$$

or

$$(1 \times 2^0) + (0 \times 2^1) + (1 \times 2^2) + (1 \times 2^3),$$

which is equivalent to 13 in the decimal system.

[The small digit to the right of the 10 or 2 is called an exponent and indicates how many times the base number is to be multiplied by itself. Thus, $10^1 = 10$, $10^2 = 10 \times 10 = 100$, $10^3 = 10 \times 10 \times 10 = 1000$, etc. Similarly, $2^1 = 2$, $2^2 = 2 \times 2 = 4$, $2^3 = 2 \times 2 \times 2 = 8$. Any number with a zero exponent is equal to unity. Thus, $10^0 = 2^0 = 1$.]

Addition in the binary system is simple. Thus,

$$0 + 0 = 0, \quad 1 + 0 = 1, \quad 1 + 1 = 10.$$

The last means: write zero and carry one. For example, add

$$
\begin{array}{cccc}
101 & 110 & 1001 & 101 \\
111 & 11 & 110 & 110 \\
\hline
1100 & 1001 & 1111 & 1011
\end{array}
$$

These examples should be checked against the table of decimal-binary equivalents.

Subtraction by addition is simplified in the binary system. The equivalent of the nines-complement of the decimal system is the ones-complement of the binary system. The ones-complement is obtained by subtracting each digit from one, which means simply that *a one becomes a zero and a zero becomes a one.* The end-around-carry is used as explained in Chapter 8. Thus, to subtract 1010 from 1110, we use the ones-complement of 1010, which is 0101. We add

$$
\begin{array}{r}
1110 \\
0101 \\
\hline
(1)\ 0011 \\
\llcorner\!\!\longrightarrow 1 \\
\hline
0100
\end{array}
$$

If the subtrahend has fewer digits (or bits) than the minuend, we supply enough zeros to give both the same number of digits. Thus, we subtract 11 from 10001. We assume 11 is 00011, and its complement is 11100. Then we add

$$
\begin{array}{r}
10001 \\
11100 \\
\hline
(1)\ 01101 \\
\llcorner\!\!\longrightarrow 1 \\
\hline
01110
\end{array}
$$

These examples should be checked against the table of equivalents.

9–2 TYPES OF CODES

In business computers it is customary to speak of *characters,* rather than bits and words. A character may be a letter of the alphabet, a number from zero to nine, or a symbol. Instead of using straight binary representation, it is more common to represent decimal numbers by *codes.* Since the codes are made up of groups of zeros and ones to represent decimal digits, they are called *binary coded decimals,* or simply, BCD.

One of the simplest codes makes use of the binary equivalent of each digit in the decimal number, and each digit is represented by four bits. Thus, the decimal 3 is binary 11, but in this code it becomes 0011. The decimal number 153 becomes 0001 0101 0011. Since it is known that four bits are needed for each digit, there is no confusion if this is all run together as 000101010011. This may seem more unwieldly than the binary equivalent for 153, which is 10011001, but it is simpler to remember since each group of four bits represents a decimal digit, and one need learn only the binary equivalents of 0 through 9.

The code just described is called a *weighted* code, since each bit in the four-bit representation has its own value or weight. Thus, the right-hand digit is weighted *one,* the next to it *two,* the third from the right *four,* and the left-hand digit *eight.* These are the powers of two as explained in the description of the binary system. The code is called the *8421 binary code,* where the numbers represent the weights. Thus, 0111 must represent $4 + 2 + 1 = 7$, 1001 represents $8 + 1 = 9$, 0101 represents $4 + 1 = 5$, etc. Other weighted codes are the 2421 binary code, and the biquinary system, which uses seven bits weighted 0543210. The *excess 3 code,* where each decimal digit is represented by the binary equivalent of a number three higher than the digit, is a nonweighted code. The representation of the decimal digits by each of these codes is shown below. Each code has its own advantages when applied to arithmetical operations in the computer.

Decimal digit	8421	2421	Biquinary 05	43210	Excess 3
0	0000	0000	10	00001	0011
1	0001	0001	10	00010	0100
2	0010	0010	10	00100	0101
3	0011	0011	10	01000	0110
4	0100	0100	10	10000	0111
5	0101	1011	01	00001	1000
6	0110	1100	01	00010	1001
7	0111	1101	01	00100	1010
8	1000	1110	01	01000	1011
9	1001	1111	01	10000	1100

Codes are needed to represent letters and other symbols as well as digits. The USS-6 code uses six bits to represent 52 different characters including the 10 decimal digits, the 26 letters of the alphabet, and assorted punctuation marks and mathematical symbols. This is shown in the following table.

Character	USS-6	Character	USS-6	Character	USS-6	Character	USS-6
0	000000	− (minus)	000101	A	010001	N	101000
1	000001	+	110000	B	010010	O	101001
2	000010	/	110001	C	010011	P	101010
3	000011	apostrophe	001111	D	010100	Q	101011
4	000100	semicolon	001110	E	011000	R	101100
5	001000	colon	010110	F	011001	S	110010
6	001001	comma	110101	G	011010	T	110011
7	001010	period	010101	H	011011	U	110100
8	001011	&	010111	I	011100	V	111000
9	001100	%	110110	J	100001	W	111001
)	000111	$	100101	K	100010	X	111010
(	001101	#	011111	L	100011	Y	111011
space	000110	*	100110	M	100100	Z	111100

The first two bits of the USS-6 code are called the *zone* and the last four are weighted code, using weights 5421. This is evident for the digits 0 through 9. For the letters of the alphabet, the code is easily translated to the IBM punched card. The 01-zone in the USS-6 code corresponds to the twelve-punch on the tab card, the 10-zone corresponds to the eleven-punch, and the 11-zone to the zero-punch (when the zero on the card is also a zone punch). The numeric portion of the USS-6 code, the 5421 portion, represents the number of the punch on the tab card for the same letter. The USS-6 code is thus a binary code corresponding to the *Hollerith code* used on cards. Another six-bit code for letters as well as numerals uses the 8421 weights instead of 5421 but is otherwise similar to USS-6. This code is called standard six-bit BCD and is used in the 1440.

The Hollerith code, as described in Chapter 5, is a method of *coding* letters, numbers, and other symbols onto a punched card so that the data can be fed into a data-processing system. The holes in punched tape are also arranged in a code. A *five-channel* code is one in which the holes can be in any one of five positions across the width of the tape. Codes are used having five, six, seven, or eight channels. Figure 9-1 shows Friden's eight-channel code for the digits and letters and a few other characters. The small feed holes between channels 3 and 4 are engaged by the driving gear to move the tape along and are not part of the code.

CHARACTER	CHANNEL NUMBERS								
	8	7	6	5	4	FEED	3	2	1
0			●			●			
1						●			●
2						●		●	
3				●		●		●	●
4						●	●		
5				●		●	●		●
6				●		●	●	●	
7						●	●	●	●
8					●	●			
9				●	●	●			●
A		●	●			●			●
B		●	●			●		●	
C		●	●	●		●		●	●
D		●	●			●	●		
E		●	●	●		●	●		●
F		●	●	●		●	●	●	
G		●	●			●	●	●	●
H		●	●		●	●			
I		●	●	●	●	●			●
J		●		●		●			●
K		●		●		●		●	
L		●				●		●	●
M		●		●		●	●		
N		●				●	●		●
O		●				●	●	●	
P		●		●		●	●	●	●
Q		●		●	●	●			
R		●			●	●			●
S			●	●		●		●	
T			●			●		●	●
U			●	●		●	●		
V			●			●	●		●
W			●			●	●	●	
X			●	●		●	●	●	●
Y			●	●	●	●			
Z			●		●	●			●
Space				●		●			
- Hyphen		●				●			
/			●	●		●			●
Stop					●	●		●	●
%		●		●	●	●		●	●
, Comma			●	●	●	●		●	●
. Period		●	●		●	●		●	●

FIG. 9-1. Punched paper-tape code. (Courtesy of IBM.)

Magnetic tape is coded in a similar manner. Instead of holes punched in the tape, magnetized dots represent the characters. Magnetic tape codes and punched-paper tape codes have not been standardized.

When numbers are represented by a straight binary number instead of a code, they can be added to yield another binary number which is their sum. However, when a code is used, there is no way of adding bits to get the correct sum every time. Therefore, it is necessary to furnish the computer a set of rules for adding, that is, a set of addition tables and rules for carrying. These rules are called *algorithms*. It should be noted that the coding and the algorithms are built into the computer, so that, in fact, it is not necessary for the operator to know what the code is or how the machine computes. However, if the machine stops because of error, a knowledge of the code is needed to find the source of the error. The particular code which is used is chosen because it requires less complicated circuitry or has other advantages in carrying out the algorithms. Thus both the 2421 code and the excess 3 code have the advantage that the nines-complement of the decimal digit can be obtained by simply changing each one to a zero and each zero to a one. This is considered a *powerful* advantage. (The word, *powerful,* to describe a computer function is used much as Hollywood uses the word, *colossal.*)

One can drive an automobile without having any idea about how the internal combustion engine works or for that matter, without knowing what is under the hood. Similarly, one can operate a computer with no knowledge of binary arithmetic or codes. However, this knowledge does help in understanding *how* the computer operates.

9–3 ERROR DETECTION

As computers age, they wear, and thus may become prone to error. The most common error is one of misreading a zero for a one, or a one for a zero. This does not happen often, but if it does it could spoil a whole computer run. It is desirable then to detect such errors when they occur and correct them before one proceeds. Special error-detecting codes are built into the computer for this purpose. These codes will not find all errors of this type but, in general, will detect most of them.

The biquinary code shown above has a "built-in" error detection capability. It can be seen that each decimal character is represented by a combination of five zeros and two ones. If a machine makes a mistake and reads a different number of ones during an operation transferring data from one point to another, this error will be detected immediately if the machine is using the biquinary code. This type of error detection is called a *parity* check. In the biquinary code, the check is for exactly two ones. Other checks may be for an even number of ones (called *even parity*) or for an odd number of ones (*odd parity*). Thus, the IBM 1401 uses the 8421 code but adds a fifth bit as a *check bit*. The 1401 then checks for odd parity. The check bit must be a zero when there is already an odd number of ones in the code, and must be a one when the number is even. For example, the check bit is zero for a 7 or 8, but is one for a 9. The IBM 1440 uses the six-bit BCD code in core storage with a seventh bit for a parity check. Every character (letters as well as numbers) is checked. When an error is detected, the machine stops until the error is corrected. It should be noted that the parity check is built into the computer. The operator does not have to know whether it is even or odd parity, nor does he have to calculate the check bit. This is done automatically.

It may be noted that the punched tape code shown in Fig. 9-1 is an odd-parity code. The number of holes representing a character is always odd. In fact, the student should check that channels 4, 3, 2, and 1 are used for the 8421 code and channels 7 and 6 for a zone, just as in the six-bit BCD code. Channel 5 is the *check* channel. A hole is placed here only to keep the number of holes an odd number.

Another type of error check is called a *validity check*. It is obvious that there are some combinations of zeros and ones which are not valid in the particular code being used, although they may be "good" numbers in other codes. If a machine is wired to recognize valid numbers, it will stop whenever an invalid number appears.

One of the most common errors is caused by an operator transposing two figures when punching a card or tape. This error can be detected by using a *check digit* which is calculated from the other digits in the number by a formula. For example, if account numbers are three-digit numbers, a typical formula might be expressed in three rules, as follows: (1) Multiply the first digit by one, the second by two, and the third by three. (2) Add the products and subtract from the next highest multiple of 10. (3) This is the check digit. Thus, if the account number is 241, we add $(2 \times 1) + (4 \times 2) + (1 \times 3) = 13$ and subtract from 20, the next multiple of 10. The check digit is therefore 7, and the number becomes 2417. Note what happens if two digits are transposed. Suppose an operator punches 2147. The computer is programmed to check every account number. When the card is fed into the machine, it calculates $(2 \times 1) + (1 \times 2) + (4 \times 3) = 16$. The check digit should be 4, and the computer stops when it reads the 7. Again, if the operator punches 2471, the machine checks $(2 \times 1) + (4 \times 2) + (7 \times 3) = 31$. This is subtracted from 40 to give a check digit of 9. The machine stops when it reads the 1 as the check digit. This capability can be programmed into the 1440 for any formula. Note that the formula given above is only an example. Actual formulas used can be simpler or much more complicated. In general, the only basic requirement is that adjacent digits be multiplied by different integers. Check digits are also called self-checking numbers.

9–4   COMPUTER LANGUAGE

Instructions as well as data must be fed into the computer, but unfortunately computers are unable to understand the written or spoken word. Thus, the instructions must be coded into numbers which cause the computers to perform the desired operations. These codes are usually too long and too complicated to learn. Instead the operator learns a special basic language. This language has a limited vocabulary but the instructions are written in this language much as they would be in English. The instructions are then fed into the machine along with a set of rules for translating them into machine language, which the computer can understand. There are many special languages which the operator can use, each with its own special applications. The languages for scientific work are not suited for business data processing and vice versa. The art of writing the instructions in the special language is called *programming*. This is the subject of the next two chapters.

BIBLIOGRAPHY

PHISTER, M., *Logical Design of Digital Computers*. New York: John Wiley and Sons, Inc., 1958. This is a middle-level engineering book. One of its chapters discusses the various common codes.

RICHARDS, R. K., *Arithmetic Operations in Digital Computers*, Princeton, N. J.: Van Nostrand, 1955. This is also a middle-level text which devotes a chapter to the structure of codes.

Each of these books has a chapter on codes as well as other information. Either one is a good addition to the computer engineer's library.

QUESTIONS

9–1
Why do many computers use a binary system of numbers instead of the decimal system of numbers?

9–2
How would you represent the number 43 in the binary system of numbers?

9–3
Do most business computers use the binary system of numbers? If not, what do they use?

9–4
How would you represent the number 4873 in the binary-coded decimal system?

9–5

How would you represent the number 583 in the binary-coded decimal system?

9–6

How would you represent the number 583 in the excess-three code?

9–7

Why is it necessary for a computer operator or a programmer to understand the particular code used by that computer?

9–8

What is meant by the statement that a certain computer has an odd-parity check? Give an example.

9–9

What distinguishes a validity check from a parity check?

9–10

Why would you ever use check digits in business data processing?

9–11

Do programmers usually program in the language the computer understands?

10

Programming

10-1 PROGRAMMING INSTRUCTIONS

Despite all the talk about giant brains, a computer is a rather *stupid* piece of equipment, if we continue the human analogy. It does operate rapidly and accurately, but it does only what it is told to do. If it makes a mistake and recognizes the mistake (error detection), it will stop, but if the source of the error is not removed, it will continue to make the same mistake over and over. Consequently, for each job, it is necessary to give the computer very explicit instructions on how to manipulate the data and what is required as output. The group of instructions is called a *program*, and the art of preparing the program is called *programming*.

In ordinary daily social conversation we frequently ask a question but expect an answer to a different question that was implied. For example, we ask a child, "May I ask your age?" The child answers, "Five," as expected. If the child were a computer, he would answer, "Yes, you may," and wait for the direct question "How old are you?" Again, the man who asks his wife "Do you remember where you put the keys to the car?" does not really expect a yes or no answer concerning his wife's memory. Since the computer answers questions exactly and has no imagination to tell what the implied question is, the programmer's job is to prepare a set of instructions in a form which will *program* the computer to furnish the required answers.

As Chapter 9 indicated, computers contain thousands of bistable elements which store the data and instructions. Therefore, every instruction must be coded in some form of ones and zeros, just as codes are used for data. The "vocabulary" of codes representing instructions is called *machine language*. In machine language each instruction is a *word*, which is a collection of numbers in whatever code is used in the machine. For example, in machine language the instruction to add may be 14. (Of course, 14 would be in one of the codes described in Chapter 9, such as

8421 or BCD.) Each instruction is located at an *address* in storage. Addresses are numbered sequentially, and each address may consist of a group of several characters. An instruction to add two numbers may be located, for example, at address number 20. The instruction might be

$$14 \quad 84 \quad 58 \quad 97 \quad 40.$$

For our example, 14 means *add*. The next two numbers are the *addresses* of the quantities to be added. Thus, the computer reads the quantity in address number 84 and duplicates it in the arithmetic unit (without removing it from address 84). Then the quantity in address 58 is read and it is also duplicated in the arithmetic unit, where it is added to what is already there. The sum is put in the accumulator. The next number, 97, is the address where the result is to be stored. Thus, the sum in the accumulator is sent to address 97, and the accumulator is cleared. In some computers which have no accumulator, such as the 1440, the addition is done in the adder and a part of storage. The last number, 40, is the address of the next instruction. Thus, each instruction consists of four parts, indicating

(1) what is to be done,
(2) where to find the data which are to be manipulated,
(3) where to put the result, and
(4) where to look for the next instruction. (If this is not given, the instructions are read sequentially.)

10–2 COMPUTER LANGUAGES

Just as the codes representing numbers differ from machine to machine, so also the machine-language instructions are different. It is not practical for a programmer to try to learn machine language. Instead, special *computer languages* have been developed which enable the programmer to instruct the machine in language which is similar to English. Each of these computer languages is designed for solving specific types of problems, so that one language is better suited to instruct a machine to solve a scientific problem, while another is particularly adapted to solving business problems. Dozens of computer languages have been invented, each with its own particular advantage. FORTRAN is the most common scientific language. (The name is an abbreviation for FORmula TRANslation.) Statements or instructions written in FORTRAN look very much like mathematical equations. At the other end of the scale is COBOL, a business language. (The name is derived from Common Business-Oriented Language.) In COBOL, instructions read like ordinary English and can be read and understood by a person not familiar with the language. The computer languages are said to be *problem-oriented*, and machine language is *machine-oriented*. A frequently used business language designed by IBM for its computers is AUTOCODER.

The computer language, of course, must be translated into machine language so that the computer can understand it. This is done by a special program called a *processor*. With each machine the computer manufacturer supplies a processor to translate the language which is to be used. If an instruction written in computer language is "ADD," the processor searches through its "dictionary" and finds the code which will make the computer add. The instruction in the problem-oriented computer program is thus translated into a new instruction in machine-oriented machine language. The computer program is usually punched on tab cards which are then placed in the input card reader of the computer. This is called the *source program*. The processor which will translate this program is placed in the same input unit, unless it is too large, in which case it may be loaded on disk packs. Each instruction in the source program is then translated by the computer itself, and the output is a new deck of cards containing the instructions in machine language. This output is called the *object program*. When an object program has been obtained for solving a specific problem, the source program is no longer needed. Whenever the same problem arises, the object program is used with new input data. For example, a simple problem may be bringing inventory up to date. The computer must be instructed to take the last inventory list, add to it the purchases during the period, and subtract the shipments. The output of the program would be a new updated list and perhaps another list indicating which items are low and need to be re-ordered. The programmer can write the instructions in COBOL, AUTO-CODER, or another language. This is the source program. These instructions are then translated into machine language (the object program). Each time that the inventory run is made, it is only necessary to furnish the computer with the object program and the latest data on purchases and shipments. The program will then instruct the machine to find the last inventory list in storage and to perform the other manipulations on the new data as required.

The simplest processor is called an *assembler*. This translates written instructions to machine language instructions on a one-for-one basis. That is, the programmer must have a good idea how the computer will operate and what each instruction must contain in code form. However, he does not have to memorize the code. The source program written for an assembly is called an *assembly program*. The language used is called an *assembly program language*. One of the common assembly program languages is *Macro Assembly Program Language* or simply MAP.

When a source program is written in FORTRAN or COBOL, each statement incorporates several machine instructions. A special type of processor, called a *compiler*, is used to translate these programs into object programs. A compiler assigns addresses for new input data, keeps track of the addresses in the object program, and writes a complete set of instructions from relatively few source-program statements. There are many computer languages, as well as FORTRAN and COBOL, which are translated by compilers. The advantage of writing a program in one of these languages is that it can be used as the source program for many different computers. Thus, if a program is written in COBOL for the IBM 1440, it is used with a COBOL compiler furnished by IBM for the 1440. The same source program can be used on a UNIVAC 1050 with a COBOL compiler furnished by UNIVAC.

The electronic computer and its peripheral equipment are termed *hardware*. Hardware includes the storage unit, arithmetic unit, control unit, and all the input and output devices used with the computer. The compiler or assembler is also supplied by the manufacturer. These "translating" programs are called *software*. In addition, software includes any object programs which have already been written for specific tasks.

10–3   PREPARING A PROGRAM

When preparing a program, the programmer must be able to see the problem as a whole as well as its component parts. He must also understand what the computer can and cannot do. In general, there are four steps in preparing a program:

1. Analyze the problem.
2. Analyze the computer.
3. Make a flow chart.
4. Translate the flow chart into instructions in computer language.

The first step, analysis of the problem, is simply determining what output is desired and what inputs are available. Thus, in a payroll problem, for example, the inputs may be hours worked for each employee and his rate of pay. The required output may be his paycheck. Files are also needed to determine deductions for various taxes, gross income to date, and other assorted facts which usually appear on the stub of the paycheck. The analysis is simply a determination of what is available and what is wanted.

The analysis of the computer is an attempt to figure out the steps the computer will have to go through to solve the problem within the limitations of what it can do. Basically, a computer can do three things:

1. transfer data from one location to another,
2. perform arithmetic calculations, and
3. make decisions on questions, such as, is A greater than B?

An analysis aimed at determining the method of attacking a problem sometimes is based on how a human would solve the problem if he had the same three capabilities. For example, suppose we have a group of different numbers which we wish to arrange in descending order. The numbers may already be in storage on disks for another purpose. For example, payroll information may be on a disk file, and one may have to determine the ten employees who earned the most money. Assuming he could read the disks, how would a human go about picking the top ten in order? One way of doing this is as follows:

1. Note the first earning figure. Call this the comparison figure.
2. Run down the list until a new figure is found which is higher than the first. Forget the first figure.
3. Continue down the list, comparing each figure in turn to the new figure.
4. Whenever a higher figure is found, the old one is dropped, and the higher one becomes the comparison figure.
5. When the bottom of the list is reached, the last comparison figure is the highest on the list. This is read out or printed out.
6. The process is repeated, ignoring the figure which was printed out. With each repetition the next highest figure is determined.

This sounds like a long procedure, but on a computer it may require only a second to determine the top ten of 1000 numbers in this manner. Note that the method requires only the abilities to compare two numbers and transfer data, both of which the computer can do. The analysis of the computer then is an attempt to determine what the computer can or cannot do and how its capabilities can be used to solve the problem.

10–4   FLOW CHART

A *flow chart* is a picture of the sequence of events and the direction of flow of information. There are many types of flow charts. In Chapter 2 we were introduced to a flow chart which indicated how data moved in an organization. Another type of flow chart is used in programming to illustrate the *procedure* which will be used to process the data. It not only shows each operation and decision which the computer performs, it also shows the sequence. In preparing a program, one may be able to proceed from the first two steps, (analysis of the problem and analysis of the computer), to the last (write the program). However, the flow chart simplifies the last step and ensures that no seemingly unimportant operation is omitted.

The *program flow chart* consists of a group of boxes of various shapes, connected in sequence by arrows indicating the direction of flow. Some

SYMBOLS

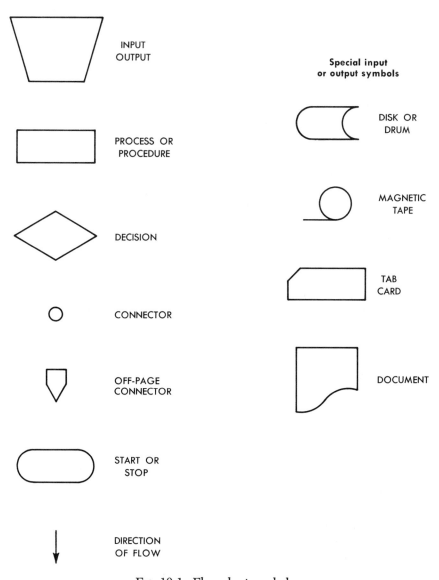

FIG. 10-1. Flow chart symbols.

of the basic symbols used are shown in Fig. 10-1. However, there is little standardization, and each programmer uses whatever symbols suit him. Some programmers, in fact, write an entire flow chart with nothing but rectangles and arrows. The trapezoid in Fig. 10-1 is used to represent either an input or an output. When the form of input is known (such as tab cards, paper tape, magnetic tape), the trapezoid may be replaced by a picture of the input device shown at the right in the figure. The process symbol, the rectangle, indicates action such as an arithmetic operation or transfer of data. The decision diamond is one of the few standardized symbols used by most programmers. It indicates that two or more possible paths are now available, depending on the comparison of two quantities. The small circle is used to break up a complicated flow chart and to keep lines from crisscrossing. A letter or number is placed in the circle, and the same letter or number is used in another circle somewhere on the same page. This indicates that the two points are connected. If the two connection points are on different pages, the off-page connector (the next symbol) is used. However, some programmers use the circle in both cases. The start or stop symbol is used at the beginning and end of the program with the appropriate word inside the symbol. Some programmers use a large circle for this. It is necessary to instruct the computer to start at the right time. It must be remembered that the program tells the machine what to do with the data, but the data are not included in the program. The computer cannot start manipulating the data until the data are fed into it. Similarly, the computer must be instructed to stop or end a program before it can start on another. The arrow is used to join the symbols and indicates direction of flow. By convention, direction of flow is from top to bottom and from left to right. Some programmers omit the arrowheads except when the flow is counter to the conventional directions.

A simpler type of flow chart is frequently used to illustrate, in general, the result of the problem analysis. This *system flow chart* indicates the inputs and desired outputs of the problem. A rectangle is used to indicate processing, just as in the program flow chart. However, the program flow chart shows every step in the procedure, whereas in the system flow chart, the rectangle is the whole process. Figure 10-2 is a *system* flow chart for updating an inventory. The present inventory file is one input, and the transactions (shipments and stock receipts) since the last inventory run is the second. These are combined: shipments are subtracted from inventory and receipts are added. The rectangle indicates that the data are processed, but in a system flow chart, there is no indication how it is done. The two outputs are a new, updated inventory file and a reorder list. The special symbols used represent the type of input or output device to be used. Thus, the symbol containing the old inventory represents a disk or drum storage unit. The new inventory symbol represents a magnetic

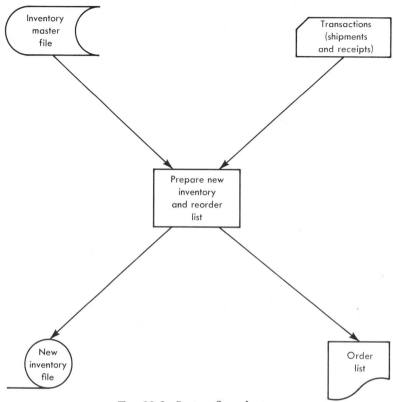

FIG. 10-2. System flow chart.

tape. The transaction input symbol represents punched cards, and the reorder list symbol represents a document. Note that trapezoids could have been used for each of the two inputs and each of the two outputs.

The reorder list is obtained by listing those items which have fallen below a certain minimum quantity. The minimum quantity for each item may be stored with that item in the master file or it may be specified in the program represented by the rectangle.

The program flow chart is much more detailed than the system flow chart since it not only indicates what is to be done, but also how to do it. Figure 10-3 is a program flow chart of the procedure for determining the ten highest numbers in a long list of numbers. The analysis of the problem and the procedure were indicated on p. 104. In our flow chart the master file containing the long list of numbers is shown as a disk file. The first symbol, marked *start*, is not necessary in our flow chart, but since the computer will have to be instructed to start (and stop), it is better to include the symbol in the flow chart so it will not be forgotten in the pro-

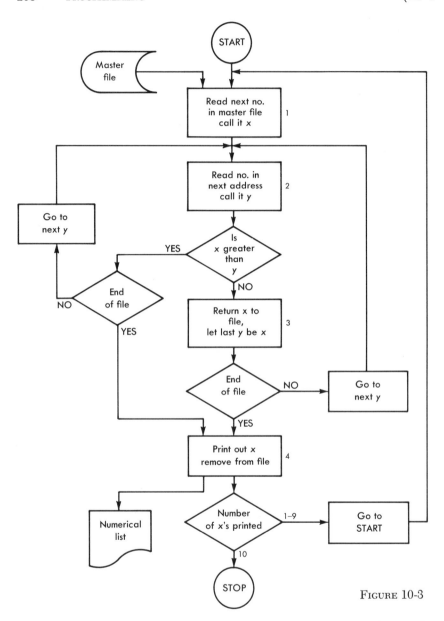

FIGURE 10-3

gram. The next symbol, box 1, indicates that the computer will read the first number in the file and call it X. (It is simpler to write X than to write "comparison figure.") The next number is read and the two are compared in the first decision symbol. Instead of writing the full statement

"Is X greater than Y?"

we can also use

$$\text{``}X > Y?\text{''}$$

which means the same thing. Another possibility is "X:Y," which means compare X to Y. In this case, instead of having YES and NO at the outputs of the diamond, we would use GREATER and LESS, respectively. Note that if X is greater than Y, we go to the next Y, which is the next number in the list, and repeat. In doing so we go through another decision symbol which asks whether we have reached the end of the list. Obviously, if we reach the end of the list, there is no next number to read. Instead we go directly to box 4, which instructs the computer to print out the value of X on a document (a sheet of paper, for example). The value of X must also be removed from the file so that it will not become a comparison figure again. To do this, when we write the program, we may first instruct the computer to move all the numbers into temporary storage. As each number is printed out, a zero is substituted for it in temporary storage, but the numbers are not destroyed in the master file.

If in the course of this comparison, a Y is found which is larger than X, the instruction in box 3 returns the X to file (where it becomes a Y), and the last Y now becomes the comparison figure and is designated X. Again, this new X is compared to each Y until the bottom of the list is reached. The value of X is printed out on the document. Note that after each print-out a decision symbol asks how many X's have been printed. If the answer is *one* to *nine*, the whole process is repeated from the beginning. If the answer is *ten*, the computer stops.

In the flow chart in Fig. 10-3, the processing rectangles were numbered for ease in referring to them. Some programmers number every box in the flow chart, and others number none. This is simply a matter of convenience and has nothing to do with the program.

The task of drawing this flow chart and writing the computer program from it is much more time consuming than the computer run, which typically may take less than a second. Once the program is written, it can be used over and over with any set of values on a disk file.

In summary then, preparing a program requires four steps: (1) analysis of the problem, determining inputs and outputs; (2) analysis of the computer; (3) preparation of a program flow chart; and (4) writing the program in computer language. The program flow chart is really a picture of the computer procedure. On the other hand, the system flow chart is really a picture of just the first step above. The fourth step, writing the program, is straightforward, but it does require a knowledge of the vocabulary and rules of a computer language. In the next chapter, the vocabulary and rules of COBOL will be explained and a sample program will be written.

BIBLIOGRAPHY

GALLER, B. A., *The Language of Computers*. New York: McGraw-Hill Book Co., 1962. Examples of flow charts describing different problems are given.

INTERNATIONAL BUSINESS MACHINES CORP., *IBM Data Processing Techniques, Flow Charting Techniques*, C20-8152. Both systems and program flow charts are defined. The symbols used in flow charts are illustrated. A number of example problems are worked.

QUESTIONS

10–1
What is meant by *"programming a computer"?*

10–2
What is meant by the term *machine language?*

10–3
Distinguish between the address of an instruction and the instruction itself.

10–4
All machine languages are the same no matter what manufacturer's computer you are referring to. *True* or *false?*

10–5
What does FORTRAN stand for and when is it used?

10–6
What does COBOL stand for and when is it used?

10–7
What do you call a program written in COBOL language? How is it converted to a program that the machine can understand?

10–8
Which is done first—making a flow chart or writing the program, and why?

10–9
What is the difference between a system flow chart as introduced in Chapter 2 and a program flow chart as introduced in this chapter?

10–10
What must be done after the programmer writes the program in computer language?

11

Writing the Program

In this chapter we shall indicate *how* a program is written and shall explain the meaning and reason behind each statement in a typical program. The purpose is not to teach you how to write a program at this point, but rather to enable you to understand what the computer does in solving a problem.

11-1 COBOL

The program flow chart is a map of the steps that the computer will go through to process the data. The written program is a series of instructions to the computer to perform these steps. In a problem-oriented language, the written program is a source program. It must be translated into a machine-oriented object program by a computer. The programmer may choose any of a number of problem-oriented languages for his source program. The COBOL language, which will be used here, was developed through a coordinated effort of computer manufacturers, computer users, and the United States Government. It was specifically designed for business data processing. Instructions written in COBOL have no resemblance to the machine-language instructions which instruct the computer, but each manufacturer can supply a COBOL compiler or processor to translate COBOL directly into machine language. The programmer does not have to know machine language or any details of the compiler.

Since COBOL is a general business language applicable to most computers, it is not as efficient as one designed specifically for a particular computer. Thus, IBM's AUTOCODER is more efficient for an IBM computer, but is unsatisfactory for a UNIVAC computer.

As in any language, the basic building blocks are a set of characters. COBOL uses 48 characters, which include the ten digits from zero to nine, the twenty-six letters of the alphabet, and the following punctuation marks and symbols:

space	(Space is considered a character.)
plus sign	$+$
minus sign or hyphen	$-$
multiplication sign	$*$ (not x, since that is a letter)
division sign	/
comma	,
period or decimal point	.
quotation mark	,
left parenthesis	(
right parenthesis	)
dollar sign	$
equal sign	=

Words in COBOL may consist of letters, numerals, special characters, or combinations of all three. (When we referred to letters and numerals earlier, we used the term *alphameric*. In most COBOL books, the term *alphanumeric* is used instead. Either term is correct.) Certain words have special meanings in COBOL and form the COBOL vocabulary. These are called *COBOL words* or *reserved words*. A partial list follows:

```
ACCEPT          DATA            JUSTIFIED       QUOTE
ADD             DIGIT
ADDRESS                         LABEL           READ
ALL             END             LOCATION        RECORD
ALPHABETIC      ENTER           LOCK            RUN
ALPHANUMERIC    ENVIRONMENT
ALTER           EQUAL           MEMORY          SECTION
AND             ERROR           MOVE            SELECT
APPLY                           MULTIPLY        SENTENCE
AREA            FD                              SOURCE-COMPUTER
ASSIGN          FILE            NEGATIVE        SPACE
AUTHOR          FILE-CONTROL    NOT             SPECIAL-NAMES
                FILLER          NUMERIC         STOP
BLANK           FIRST                           SUBTRACT
BLOCK                           OBJECT-COMPUTER
                GO              OBJECT-PROGRAM  TO
CHARACTER       GREATER         OPEN
CHECK                           OUTPUT          VALUE
CLASS           IDENTIFICATION
CLOSE           IF              PERFORM         WORDS
COBOL           INPUT           PICTURE         WORKING-STORAGE
COMPUTE         INPUT-OUTPUT    POINT           WRITE
COPY            I-O-CONTROL     PROCEED
                                PROCEDURE       ZERO
```

The compiler will not distinguish between singular and plural forms. However, plural forms may be used to make the instructions "sound better."

It is permissible to use any combination of letters and digits to form *names*. A name is used simply as a convenient way of referring to something again and again. Instead of calling it "it" or "thing," it is easier to give a file or a record or an item to be processed a name, so that it can be referred to later. The following rules apply to the forming of names:

1. Names may contain from one to thirty characters.
2. Names must not contain blanks.
3. Names may contain hyphens, but may not start or end with a hyphen.
4. In general, a name must contain at least one alphabetic character.

The English language has rules for combining words to make sentences and combining sentences to make paragraphs. A COBOL program must also be written according to strict rules which are analogous to the rules of grammar. The rules of COBOL and their exceptions are the subject matter of whole textbooks, a few of which are referred to at the end of this chapter. Some of these rules will be illustrated in the examples which follow.

11–2 THE COBOL PROGRAM

Let us take a typical problem and follow it through from the statement of the problem to the written program. The Buttons and Bows Company has a large inventory of supplies it sells to other companies, as well as tools, cloth, and other items used in manufacturing its products. Each type of item is given a stock number which consists of the letters "BB" followed by a hyphen and five digits. Thus, the number BB-00126 is the 126th item in the inventory list. It might represent envelopes the company uses for billing, pink bows for sale to the dressmaking industry, or needles to be used by the BB Company in the manufacturing process. The entire inventory list from BB-00001 to the highest number (which, for our example, we will assume to be BB-01234) is stored sequentially in a disk file. In each file location, the following information is stored: the inventory number, the quantity of that item in stock at the time of the last inventory check, and the *reorder threshold*. The reorder threshold indicates the minimum quantity that should be maintained in inventory. When the actual quantity of a particular item falls below this threshold, the item should be reordered to bring the stock up to an acceptable level (perhaps, two or three times the threshold). The problem to be considered is that of checking the inventory of the Buttons and Bows Company so that the list stored in the disk file is up to date and so that all items which have fallen below threshold can be reordered.

Figure 11-1 is a system flow chart of the problem showing the inputs and required outputs. If we know the form of our input and output, we

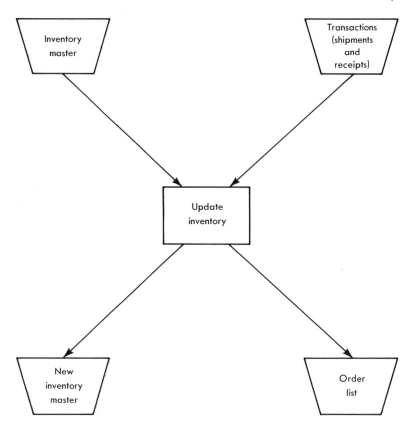

Fig. 11-1. System flow chart for inventory check.

can use the special input-output symbols instead of trapezoids, as we did in Fig. 10-2. To make a program flow chart we must analyze how the computer will solve the problem. Before the problem reaches the computer, some of the information is put on punched cards and is processed separately. In this example, each time an item is drawn out of stock, a card is punched indicating the item number in the first eight columns and the quantity drawn out in columns 19–24. Each time stock is replenished, a card is punched indicating the item number in columns 1–8 and the quantity added in columns 11–16. Note that the item number occupies the same columns on both types of cards. We will call the withdrawals from stock SHIPMENTS (regardless of where they are going) and the additions to stock, RECEIPTS. The cards could be punched by an operator using an IBM 26 keypunch. They are called *transaction cards*.

When it is time to make the new inventory check, all the cards representing shipments and receipts, since the last inventory check, are fed into an IBM 83 sorter and arranged numerically by item number in the first eight columns. It is then necessary to obtain *summary cards.* Each summary card will contain the item number in columns 1–8, the sum of all receipts for that item in columns 11–16, and the sum of all shipments for that item in columns 19–24. There is now *one* summary card for each item that was changed during the month. To obtain the summary cards, the transaction cards can be fed into an IBM 407, which is connected to an IBM 519 for summary punching. If the volume is large, the computer system itself would be used for both the sorting and summary punching. The summary cards, in numerical order by item number, are now ready to be fed into the card reader in the computer.

Figure 11-2 is a program flow chart and indicates the result of the analysis of the computer; that is, it shows how the computer will be used to solve the problem. The dashed rectangle at the upper right indicates that some processing, which resulted in the summary cards, has already occurred. The inputs to our program are shown in boxes 1 and 2; the outputs are shown in boxes 3 and 4. These agree with those shown in the system flow chart of Fig. 11-1. Beginning at start, we note that the first instruction is to read the "next" summary card. Here *next* means *first,* since none have been read yet. This card will have three numbers, the item number, the receipts, and the shipments. These three numbers will be fed into the flow chart later in different places. The next instruction is to read the "next" inventory record. Again this means *first* record.

A *record* is a unit within a file. If cards are used as a file, each card is a record. If a disk file, magnetic tape, or other storage device is used, a record is a complete description of an item. Thus, in our example, an inventory record in the disk file consists of the item number, the quantity in stock, and the reorder threshold. A transaction record on a card consists of the item number, the receipts, and the shipments. In COBOL, as we shall see, a record is called a *first level* or *level* 01. The items that make up a record are level 02, and they can be further subdivided into 03, 04, etc. In our example, the tab card and the disk file record are both level 01. The item number, item quantity, reorder threshold, receipts, and shipments are all level 02.

Box 7 asks whether the item numbers on the card and inventory record are alike. If not, there were no transactions for the item in that inventory record, since both cards and inventory file were in numerical order at the start. In this case, we must simply place the unchanged inventory record in the new master file and go on to the next inventory record. Box 8 is the instruction to list in the new file. Before we return to read a new inventory record, we ask in box 9 whether we have reached the end of the list (the number is BB-01234). If we have, we stop the program; if not, we return to box 6. This is indicated by the connector symbol designated

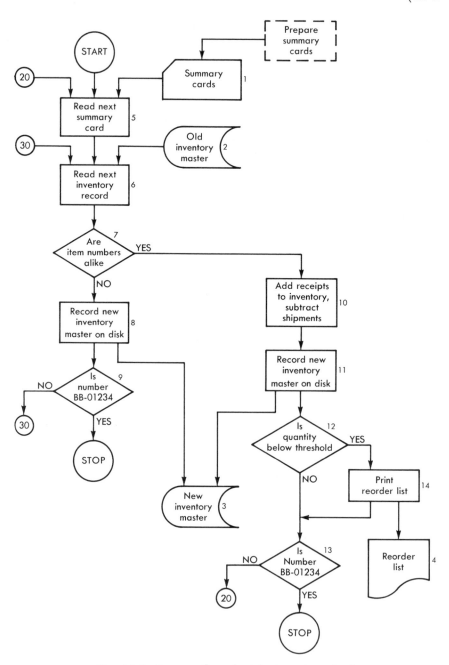

FIG. 11-2. Program flow chart for inventory check.

30 in both places. If we wish, we can also connect the points on the diagram directly.

Returning to box 7, if the item numbers *are* alike, we proceed to box 10, which combines the transactions and the old inventory record. The new record is recorded as before. Box 12, a decision symbol, checks the new quantity against the threshold level. If it is low, the item is printed on the reorder list. In either case, we go to box 13, which asks whether we have reached the end of the list. If we have, we stop, as before. If not, we need a new summary card as well as a new inventory record; so we return to start, indicated by the connectors marked 20. (Any numbers can be used inside the connector symbols.) The flow chart will be used to help write the program.

11–3   PROGRAM DIVISIONS

A COBOL program consists of four parts, called *divisions*. The first is the *Identification Division,* which contains the name of the program, the name of the programmer, the date it is written, and any remarks that the programmer wishes to add for his own information.

The second division is called the *Environment Division.* It consists of two sections. The *Configuration Section* describes the computer or computers to be used and defines any special names which will be used. The *Input-Output Section* names the files which will be used and indicates what they will be called. Both the Identification Division and the Environment Division have little effect on the computer operation, but they must be included in the program.

The third division is called the *Data Division.* Here the files are described, including the number of characters in each record. If records in files are to be moved into temporary storage during the computer operation, these *Work Areas* for temporary storage are described, indicating which records will occupy them and how many characters will be needed. Using temporary storage as a work area is something like using scratch paper for solving problems.

The last division is called the *Procedure Division.* This contains the instructions indicated by the flow chart. All four divisions must be present in the program in the indicated order.

11–4   COBOL FORM

It is possible to scribble the program on ordinary paper. However, after the program is written, it is usually punched on cards to be fed into the computer. To simplify the work of the keypunch operator and to reduce the chances of making a mistake, the program is usually printed in capital letters on a special form. Figure 11-3 illustrates the COBOL program for the flow chart of Fig. 11-2. The student should disregard the program at this point and look only at the form. Since the program will be punched on cards which have 80 columns, the program is written on paper ruled to indicate these columns with each character placed in a box for its respective column. Each line of the program will be punched onto a separate tab card. The last eight columns in a COBOL program are usually used for identification, so that an individual card can be checked in these columns to see to what deck (program) it belongs. The identification can be numeric or alphameric, but it is usually a descriptive word. Since the same identification will be used on all the cards in the program, it is not repeated on each line. Instead the form is only 72 columns wide. The last eight columns are indicated near the upper right in a box marked *Identification*. Whatever is put in these boxes is punched on every card. In our example, we are using "INV-CK" for "inventory check." As shown, these six characters are placed in columns 74–79, with 73 and 80 left blank. On some forms, every column is numbered from 4 to 72 and on others, like the one shown in the figure, every fourth, or fifth, or even tenth column is numbered.

The first three columns represent the page number. The first page is 001, and conceivably it could go as high as 999. On every card made from page 001, 001 will be punched in the first three columns of the first line and will be understood to refer to every entry on that page. Thus it is not necessary to repeat this all the way down the page.

Note that the keypunch operator's work is simplified by the duplicating feature on the keypunch program card. After the first card is punched, duplicating of the first three and last eight columns of the next card is done automatically.

Note that the program is written in capitals for ease in reading and to reduce the possibility of error. The letter O is written with a slash through it, Ø, to distinguish it from zero, which is simply 0. The letter I always has bars on top and bottom to distinguish it from the numeral one. The letter Z is written with a bar through it, Ƶ, to distinguish it from the numeral 2.

11–5   WRITING A COBOL PROGRAM

Figure 11-3(a) contains both the Identification and Environment Divisions. The format for writing COBOL will be described using this program as an example. The program is written in sentences and paragraphs. However, a paragraph must begin with a title and may contain nothing more. A paragraph and a major subdivision must begin at column 8. This is called *Margin A* and is indicated by an A on the form. Minor subdivisions and all continuations begin at column 12, called *Margin B*.

Columns 4–6 are used for the serial number. It is common practice to begin with 010 on each page and continue by tens (020, 030, etc.). If the programmer has an afterthought, he can then write an instruction 025 or 033, for example, to indicate that it falls between two of those already written. Thus, it is not necessary to renumber the whole program. The additional instruction can follow the entire program, since after the cards are punched they can be sorted numerically.

The first line of the program is the title IDENTIFICATIØN DIVISIØN. Note that it begins at column 8 and is followed by a period. Each title and each sentence must end in a period. The names of the divisions and sections must be on separate lines with no other words on the line. Other titles, however, may be followed by statements on the same line, provided that the title is followed by a period and at least one space. The second line also begins at column 8. It has the title PRØGRAM-ID. The name of the program, INVENTØRY CØNTRØL, appears on the same line. Note the period at the end. If there is no period at the end of a line, the next card is considered as part of the same instruction. The third line has the title AUTHØR, followed by the author's name, A. Programmer. There are two spaces between the period after AUTHØR and the author's name. There must be at least one, but there is no limit on the number of spaces which can follow a period. The fourth line is the date. The fifth line contains remarks. These may be explanations for the person using the program in the programmer's absence. Note that this instruction uses two lines and thus will be punched on two cards. Since no afterthoughts can result in a card between the two, these two lines are numbered consecutively, 050 and 051. The card for line 050 has no period at the end, and hence the compiler interprets both lines together. Line 051, being a continuation, begins at column 12. In general, the Identification Division is short and self-explanatory.

The Environment Division begins on line 060. The space between this and the preceding division is only for the programmer's convenience and is not necessary. The titles ENVIRØNMENT DIVISIØN, CØNFIGURATIØN SECTIØN, and INPUT-ØUTPUT SECTIØN must all appear on separate lines as indicated, with nothing else on the lines. Each must end in a period. Remember that the Environment Division is made up of these two sections.

The first line in the Configuration Section after the title must indicate the SØURCE CØMPUTER. This is the computer which will take the source program and compiler and produce the object program. The next line indicates the ØBJECT CØMPUTER, which will run the object program. In most cases, the same computer will be used for both. In lines 080 and 090, the IBM 1440 is indicated. Additional storage, if used, can be indicated on the same lines.

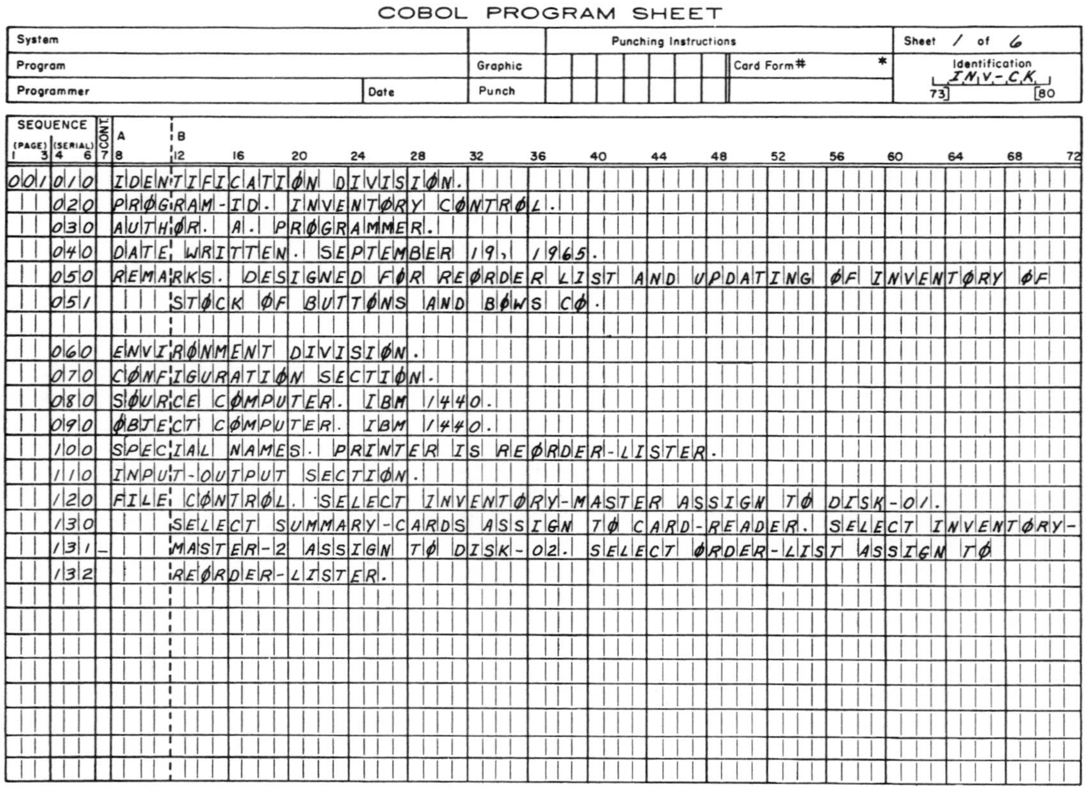

COBOL PROGRAM SHEET

System

Program

Programmer   Date

Punching Instructions

Graphic
Punch

Card Form #   *

Sheet 1 of 6

Identification
I M V - C K
73   80

```
SEQUENCE
(PAGE) (SERIAL)
001 010  IDENTIFICATION DIVISION.
    020  PROGRAM-ID. INVENTORY CONTROL.
    030  AUTHOR. A. PROGRAMMER.
    040  DATE WRITTEN. SEPTEMBER 19, 1965.
    050  REMARKS. DESIGNED FOR REORDER LIST AND UPDATING OF INVENTORY OF
    051       STOCK OF BUTTONS AND BOWS CO.
    060  ENVIRONMENT DIVISION.
    070  CONFIGURATION SECTION.
    080  SOURCE COMPUTER. IBM 1440.
    090  OBJECT COMPUTER. IBM 1440.
    100  SPECIAL NAMES. PRINTER IS REORDER-LISTER.
    110  INPUT-OUTPUT SECTION.
    120  FILE CONTROL. SELECT INVENTORY-MASTER ASSIGN TO DISK-01.
    130       SELECT SUMMARY-CARDS ASSIGN TO CARD-READER. SELECT INVENTORY-
    131-      MASTER-2 ASSIGN TO DISK-02. SELECT ORDER-LIST ASSIGN TO
    132       REORDER-LISTER.
```

FIG. 11-3 (a) A COBOL program.

COBOL PROGRAM SHEET

System ___

Program ___

Programmer ___ Date ___

Punching Instructions

Graphic ___ Punch ___

Card Form# ___ *___

Sheet 2 of 6

Identification _IMV–C.K._ (73–80)

SEQUENCE (PAGE) (SERIAL)	A	B	
002 010	DATA DIVISION.		
020	FILE SECTION.		
030	FD INVENTORY MASTER		
040	RECORD CONTAINS 24 CHARACTERS.		
050	BLOCK CONTAINS 4 RECORDS.		
060	DATA RECORD IS INV-MSTR.		
070	RECORDING MODE IS BINARY HIGH DENSITY.		
080	LABEL RECORDS ARE OMITTED.		
090	01 INV-MSTR.		
100	02 ITEM-NUMBER-1 PICTURE X(8).		
110	02 FILLER PICTURE X(2).		
120	02 ORDER-THRESHOLD-1 PICTURE X(6).		
130	02 FILLER PICTURE X(2).		
140	02 ITEM-QUANTITY-1 PICTURE X(6).		
150	FD SUMMARY-CARDS.		
160	RECORD CONTAINS 80 CHARACTERS.		
170	DATA RECORD IS SUM-CDS.		
180	BLOCK CONTAINS 1 RECORD.		
190	LABEL RECORDS ARE OMITTED.		

FIGURE 11-3 (b)

COBOL PROGRAM SHEET

System

Program

Programmer   Date

Graphic   Punch

Punching Instructions

Card Form #   *

Sheet 3 of 6

Identification INV-CK

SEQUENCE	CONT	A	B	
0103010		01	SUM-CD.	
020			02	ITEM-NUMBER-12 PICTURE X(8).
030			02	FILLER PICTURE X(2).
040			02	ITEM-QUANTITY-12A PICTURE X(6).
050			02	FILLER PICTURE X(2).
060			02	ITEM-QUANTITY-12S PICTURE X(6).
070			02	FILLER PICTURE X(56).
080		FD	INVENTORY-MASTER-2.	
090			RECORD CONTAINS 24 CHARACTERS.	
100			BLOCK CONTAINS 4 RECORDS.	
110			DATA RECORD IS INV-MSTR-2.	
120			RECORDING MODE IS BINARY HIGH DENSITY.	
130			LABEL RECORDS ARE OMITTED.	
140		01	INV-MSTR-2.	
150			02	ITEM-NUMBER-3 PICTURE X(8).
160			02	FILLER PICTURE X(2).
170			02	ORDER-THRESHOLD-3 PICTURE X(6).
180			02	FILLER PICTURE X(2).
190			02	ITEM-QUANTITY-3 PICTURE X(6).

FIGURE 11-3 (c)

COBOL PROGRAM SHEET

System						
Program			Punching Instructions			Sheet 4 of 6
Programmer		Date	Graphic	Punch	Card Form #	*
						Identification I N V - C K (73-80)

SEQUENCE (PAGE 1-3) (SERIAL 4-6)	CONT 7	A 8	B 12	16	20	24	28	32	36	40	44	48
01 04 010		FD	ORDER-LIST.									
020			RECORD CONTAINS 120 CHARACTERS.									
030			DATA RECORD IS ORD-LIST.									
040			LABEL RECORDS ARE OMITTED.									
050			BLOCK CONTAINS 1 RECORD.									
060		01	ORD-LIST.									
070			02 ITEM-NUMBER-4 PICTURE X(8).									
080			02 FILLER PICTURE X(2).									
090			02 ORDER-THRESHOLD-4 PICTURE X(6).									
100			02 FILLER PICTURE X(2).									
110			02 ITEM-QUANTITY-4 PICTURE X(6).									
120			02 FILLER PICTURE X(96).									
130			WORKING STORAGE SECTION.									
140		01	WORK-AREA-1.									
150			02 ITEM-NUMBER-5 PICTURE X(8).									
160			02 FILLER PICTURE X(2).									
170			02 ORDER-THRESHOLD-5 PICTURE X(6).									
180			02 FILLER PICTURE X(2).									
190			02 ITEM-QUANTITY-5 PICTURE X(6).									

FIGURE 11-3 (d)

COBOL PROGRAM SHEET

System							Sheet 5 of 6
Program				Punching Instructions	Card Form #	*	
Programmer		Date	Graphic				Identification: I M V – C X
			Punch				73 [80]

SEQUENCE (PAGE) (SERIAL)	CONT. A	B														
1 3 4 6 7 8	12	16	20	24	28	32	36	40	44	48	52	56	60	64	68	72
010 050 01	WORK-AREA-12.															
020	02 ITEM-NUMBER-6 PICTURE X(18).														
030	02 FILLER PICTURE X(2).														
040	02 ITEM-QUANTITY-6A PICTURE X(6).														
050	02 FILLER PICTURE X(2).														
060	02 ITEM-QUANTITY-6S PICTURE X(6).														
070	CONSTANT SECTION.														
080	01 LAST-INVENTORY-ITEM, VALUE BB-01234.													

FIGURE 11-3 (e)

COBOL PROGRAM SHEET

System				Punching Instructions				Sheet 6 of 6
Program				Graphic				Identification I N V - C K
Programmer		Date		Punch		Card Form #	*	73 80

SEQUENCE (PAGE) (SERIAL)	CONT A B	
006010		PROCEDURE DIVISION.
020		OPEN INPUT INVENTORY-MASTER, SUMMARY-CARDS.
030		OPEN OUTPUT INVENTORY-MASTER-2, ORDER-LIST.
040		READ COLUMNS 11-24 OF SUMMARY-CARDS INTO WORK-AREA-12.
050		READ INVENTORY-MASTER INTO WORK-AREA-1.
060		READ-1. READ NEXT RECORD IN WORK-AREA-2.
070		READ-2. READ NEXT RECORD IN WORK-AREA-1.
080		IF INVENTORY-NUMBER-5 EQUALS INVENTORY-NUMBER-6 GO TO 100.
090		GO TO 130.
100		CALCULATIONS. ADD ITEM-QUANTITY-6A TO ITEM-QUANTITY-5. SUBTRACT
101		ITEM-QUANTITY-6S FROM ITEM-QUANTITY-5.
110		IF ITEM-NUMBER-5 IS LESS THAN LAST-INVENTORY-ITEM GO TO
111		READ-1.
120		GO TO WRITE.
130		IF ITEM-NUMBER-5 IS LESS THAN LAST-INVENTORY-ITEM GO TO
131		READ-2.
140		WRITE.
150		IF ITEM-QUANTITY-5 IS LESS THAN ORDER-THRESHOLD-5 WRITE
151		ORD-LIST.
160		WRITE INVI-MSTR-2 FROM WORK-AREA-1.
170		FINISH.
180		CLOSE INVENTORY-MASTER WITH LOCK, SUMMARY-CARDS, INVENTORY-
171-		MASTER-2 WITH LOCK, ORDER-LIST.
190		STOP RUN.

FIGURE 11-3 (f)

Following the computer descriptions, the Configuration Section also lists special names. Line 100 indicates that whenever the name REØRDER-LISTER appears in the program, it refers to the printer. If there were other special names, they could be listed on succeeding lines, beginning in column 12.

The Input-Output Section begins with the title on line 110. Line 120 begins with the name FILE-CØNTROL and then describes the two inputs and two outputs. The two inputs are the old inventory and the summary cards. These will be described in detail when we discuss the Data Division. The format for file-control is shown in lines 120 and following. The instruction is always SELECT . . . ASSIGN . . . Thus, the old inventory, which is called INVENTØRY-MASTER, is assigned to a disk file called DISK-01. We can also interpret this to mean that whatever is in DISK-01 is now called INVENTØRY-MASTER. The summary cards are assigned to the card reader. The outputs are also assigned. The new inventory list will appear on DISK-2 which is now called INVENTØRY-MASTER-2. The order list will appear on the REØRDER-LISTER, which (from line 100) is the special name for the printer. As before, lines 130, 131, and 132 will not be separated and are thus numbered consecutively. Note the hyphen in column 7 of line 131 which indicates that the first word on the card is a continuation of a hyphen at the end of the preceding card.

The Data Division is usually the largest part of the written program. In our program we use four program sheets for it. The first line of Fig. 11-3(b) is simply the title. The Data Division has three sections: (1) the *file section*, (2) the *work storage section*, and (3) the *constant section*. As with the title of the division, the title of each of these sections begins at column 8 and stands alone. Under file section, each file is described. The description begins with the letters FD, which mean *file description* and each record is described by the level number 01. Each part of the record is described with appropriate level numbers which are higher numerically the less important they are. The FD and 01 descriptions begin at column 8 and the lower levels (higher level numbers) begin at column 12.

Line 030 has the title FD INVENTØRY-MASTER, and the following lines will describe this file. Reading these lines, we see that a record has 24 characters and that a *block* contains 4 records. A block is a group of records which are read and then processed. The computer must transfer records from file storage to the work storage area. It can transfer one record, process it, and then go on to the next, or it can transfer several in a block, process them in turn, and then go on to the next block. The larger the block, the faster will be the procedure. However, large blocks require larger work storage areas. For a medium-size computer like the 1440, a block of about 100 characters is a convenient size. Line 060 indicates that we will refer to the record as INV-MSTR, to conserve storage space. Line 070 indicates the storage mode in the file. Remember, in the environment division we had already indicated that this file would be on disk file, called DISK-01. If more than one storage mode is available, we select one according to the manufacturer's instructions. Line 080 referring to label records is necessary in the program. *Label records* are used on magnetic tape to identify tapes quickly. They are not used here, and the computer must be so instructed or it might try to find a label record.

Line 090 is level 01 (that is, a record). Since it has the title INV-MSTR, we know that the next lines will describe the record mentioned in line 060. Each item of this record is given the level 02 and is described in the next five lines. Line 100 describes ITEM-NUMBER-1. The word PICTURE in COBOL means that what follows looks like the item being described. The letter X after picture means that any character in the COBOL list of characters can be used. The numeral in parentheses indicates how many characters are in the description. Thus line 100 says that in the old inventory list (INV-MSTR), the item number consists of eight characters which may be any COBOL characters. There are many symbols used instead of X. A few important ones follow. The number 9 instead of X indicates a numeral. Thus, PICTURE 9 (5) means the item consists of five numerals. The letter A indicates a letter of the alphabet or a space. Instead of using parentheses, it is permissible to repeat the picture symbol the required number of times. Thus, PICTURE X (8) for the item number could be PICTURE XXXXXXXX. Since we know that it consists of two letters, a hyphen, and five digits, it could also be PICTURE AAX99999. However, we are concerned mainly with how much space will be required, so the form of line 100 is preferred. The word FILLER means space. Thus, lines 110 and 130 indicate simply that there are two spaces. The description of INV-MSTR contained in lines 090 to 140 simply says that the 24 characters indicated in line 040 consist of eight for the item number, followed by two spaces, then six for the order threshold, followed by two more spaces, then six for the quantity of that particular item in stock. Note that the term *item number* is used in four places, on each input and each output. In order to differentiate, a digit is placed after the name. Thus, ITEM-NUMBER-1 means an item number in the old inventory file; ITEM-NUMBER-2 is on a summary card, etc. Similarly, other names have numeral suffixes to distinguish them.

Lines 150–190 contain a file description of the summary cards. Each card has 80 columns, which accounts for line 160. It is usual to process one card at a time, so a block contains only one record. The record is described in Fig. 11-3(c), lines 010–070. The first eight columns contain the item number, followed by two spaces and six columns for receipts. After another two spaces, six more are used for shipments. In the terms ITEM-

QUANTITY-2A and ITEM-QUANTITY-2S, the A and S at the ends are mnemonic aids to indicate that these must be added to and subtracted from ITEM-QUANTITY-1 in the old inventory.

Lines 080–190 describe the new inventory file. Except for the numeral suffixes on the names, it is the same as the old inventory file described on page 002, lines 030–140. In Fig. 11-3(d), the order list is described. Since the printer usually prints 120 characters to a line, this number is used for the record-size, but the last 96 spaces are left blank. This section should be self-explanatory.

The two "scratch pads," the work areas, are described in the WØRK-ING-STØRAGE SECTIØN. See Fig. 11-3(d) and (e). As we shall see in the Procedure Division, the old inventory master will be placed in work-area-1, and the records on the summary cards in work-area-2. The areas then must have room to accept the data records. The description will be similar to the description of the record which will move into the area. It is not necessary to reserve space for the 56 unused columns on the card.

The constant section tells us that whenever LAST-INVENTØRY-ITEM appears on the program, we know it means BB-01234. If, at a later date, more items are added to the inventory list, it is only necessary to make a change on this one card.

The Procedure Division is shown in Fig. 11-3(f). Line 020 is an instruction to connect the inputs to the computer and line 030 opens the outputs. Without instructions to open the files, it would be impossible to gain access to them. Lines 040 and 050 move the input data records to the work areas. The work areas in the 1440 are usually in the core storage section. Thus, the records on the summary cards and the records in the inventory file would be moved to the core memory by these instructions. However, if the core storage is not large enough, it is possible to add other storage units for work areas. Line 060 is an instruction to read the next summary card which is now in WØRK-AREA-2. This instruction corresponds to box 5 on the flow chart of Fig. 11-2, and the next instruction corresponds to box 6. The next two lines correspond to the decision box 7 in Fig. 11-2. If the numbers are alike (the YES answer in the figure), line 080 instructs the computer to skip to the calculations in line 100, which corresponds to box 10 in Fig. 11-2. Line 100 instructs the computer to add receipts *to* the quantity in the inventory master and to subtract shipments. These changes are performed to the number in WØRK-AREA-1 called ITEM-QUANTITY-5. Thus, as we go through the program, the record in WØRK-AREA-1 is changed from the old inventory to the new, item by item. This is a different procedure from that indicated on the flow chart, where each item was deposited in the new file as it was updated. In the written program, we will get a completely new inventory in the work area before the computer writes anything.

When the instructions reach line 080, if the number of the inventory record is not the same as that of the summary card, the computer does not skip to line 100. Instead it proceeds with the next instruction, line 090, which makes it skip to line 130. Note that line 110 corresponds to box 13 in Fig. 11-2 and line 130 corresponds to box 9, with a NØ decision in both cases. If the answer is YES in either case, the last number has been reached. The next instruction in both cases is to skip to line 150 to write out the order test and move the new inventory from WØRK-AREA-1 to the ouput disk file.

The concluding instructions disconnect the input and output devices from the computer. The words WITH LØCK mean that a protective device is used to prevent these files from being erased accidentally. The last instruction is STØP RUN.

In this program, the use of work areas eliminated the problem of erasing numbers in the file. It also simplified the program, since the steps indicated in boxes 8 and 11 could be combined in one step after all the numbers were read. In writing the program, then, it is important to know the computer's capacity and how it will operate.

In summary, the written COBOL program is divided into four main parts:

1. The Identification Division, which identifies the program and author;
2. The Environment Division, which describes the computer and the peripheral input-output equipment;
3. The Data Division, which describes the files and records to be used and indicates temporary work storage areas; and
4. The Procedure Division, which describes the program flow chart.

Although the program has a rigid format, it is easily read and understood, because it follows normal language structure. Outside of names, the vocabulary is limited, but sufficient for all business processing.

What if the programmer makes a mistake? The computer will then turn out erroneous answers. Unfortunately, programmers do make mistakes, and it is important to correct them before time and money are spent on computer runs. To check a program for mistakes, it is usually run with known data, so that the correct computer output is known beforehand. Intermediate results are also known and can be read out of the computer as required. If the answer is obtained at any intermediate point, the program can be checked to find the source of the error. This is called *debugging* the program. It is usually faster to debug the program by checking it on the computer than to go over it painstakingly item by item.

BIBLIOGRAPHY

CHAPIN, NED, *Programming Computers for Business Applications.* New York: McGraw-Hill Book Co., 1961. This business-oriented book discusses how to prepare programs for the cases where (a) the problem is carefully designed in advance, and (b) the programmer must develop the problem.

LEDLEY, R. S., *Programming and Utilizing Digital Computers.* New York: McGraw-Hill Book Co., 1962. This text covers machine languages, automatic programming languages (e.g., ALGOL and COBOL), and data processing techniques (e.g., Boolean algebra, searching, sorting, etc.).

McCRACKEN, D. D., *A Guide to COBOL Programming.* New York: McGraw-Hill Book Co., 1963. This is an introduction to COBOL presented in a general form. All important statements are discussed and three case studies are presented.

McCRACKEN, D. D., *Digital Computer Programming.* New York: John Wiley and Sons, 1957. The reader must be prepared to start at the beginning and work up to the described programming concepts. Interpretive, executive, and compiling routines are briefly explained.

McCRACKEN, D. D., H. WEISS and TSAI-HUA LEE, *Programming Business Computers.* New York: John Wiley and Sons, 1959. Among other important topics, this book covers the structure of files, flow charting, data-processing equipment, and programming.

QUESTIONS

11–1
Why is the COBOL language so widely used in programming computers?

11–2
Comment on the statement "COBOL is a language that the computer can interpret to carry out and process the program."

11–3
What is the purpose of using names in writing a computer program in the COBOL language?

11–4
When the computer processor (either an assembler or compiler) finishes converting the source program to a machine language program, the punch unit punches out a deck of cards containing the machine language program. What is this deck called?

11–5
What is the distinction between a record and a file?

11–6

What is the significance of a period (.) in COBOL programming?

11–7

Why is the COBOL programming language divided into four parts?

11–8

What is meant by the *vocabulary* of the COBOL programming language?

11–9

Can a programmer use one of the *vocabulary* words as a *name* in his program?

12

Choosing a Computer

12–1 REASONS FOR INSTALLING A COMPUTER

The description of operation and procedures in Chapters 8 through 11 assumes that a computer and an electronic data-processing system are in use. But there is always the first step. At what point therefore does a company decide to shift from manual or mechanical data processing to EDP? When this decision is made, how does management determine which of the many computers on the market is best suited to the task?

There are generally three possible reasons for installing electronic data processing. These are: (1) to reduce clerical costs, (2) to increase productivity, and (3) to aid management in decision making. The first two reasons are very clear cut. Costs of bookkeeping operations and production can be calculated both before and after a computer is added and the savings can be determined. It has been found, however, that the savings and increased profits that are obtained because the computer introduces scientific management techniques are far greater in the long run than the savings in clerical costs. The science of studying and analyzing management problems in order to arrive at optimum decisions is called *Operations Research* or *OR*. This is a very broad subject, taught as a separate discipline, but for the purpose of giving an example, we will list a few operations research techniques in which the computer plays a part.

Management of inventory is a problem ideally suited to the computer. Maintaining an inventory requires capital expenditure to buy the items which will be stocked. This is one of the investments that a company must make. A company's profit is related to the investment and is called *return on investment*. Obviously, if the investment can be reduced without cutting the profit, the return on investment (expressed as a percentage) is increased. In addition, it frees investment capital for possible expansion. Another advantage gained by reducing inventory is a tax savings, since companies are required to pay a tax on the inventory they maintain. It therefore is important for a company to maintain as small an inventory as possible, but still have enough stock to do business. The numbers and kinds of items which are to be kept in stock are a management decision, which can be solved with a computer. In the first place, the computer can be fed all the facts concerning possible and probable withdrawals from stock and can make a far more accurate prediction of the correct number of each item that is to be kept in inventory. In the second place, and more important, the computer can check inventory in a matter of seconds or even make a continuous running check on it, signaling quickly what items need be reordered. Thus, it is possible to keep a low inventory and order more frequently, instead of maintaining a large stock to tide the company over until the next inventory check is taken.

Another OR technique is *linear programming*, which was mentioned in the first chapter. In a typical problem, there are several machines, several people, and several tasks to be done. Knowing how long it takes each machine and each person to perform each job makes it possible to calculate the time required to perform the total job with specific assignments of tasks to people and equipment. In a few seconds, the computer can check every possible combination and determine which will get the job done in the least time. This may require thousands of iterations or repetitions, a mammoth task for a human, but a cinch for a computer.

Queuing theory is another OR technique. As an oversimplified example, let us assume that in a supermarket there are lines of housewives waiting to be checked out. How many clerks should the supermarket have? If there are enough so that there will be no housewives waiting, then in offpeak hours, many will be idle. If there are too few, housewives will take their business elsewhere, or it will be impossible to check out all the housewives during working hours. Using queuing theory the computer can determine how many clerks should be available at various hours.

12-2   WHAT KIND OF COMPUTER?

Assuming that the decision has been made to install a computer, the next question to be answered is what type or model it should be. This requires a study of the system. *Systems analysis* is the science of breaking down a system into its component parts to determine what can be accomplished. *Systems synthesis* is the science of putting together components to make a system which can perform specific tasks. Both analysis and synthesis are required here. First the problem must be analyzed. What files must be maintained? How large are they? The answers determine the type of storage unit and the size of storage. What inputs will be used and what form will they be in? What are the required outputs? The answers to these two questions determine the input-output units to be used.

When the decision to buy (or rent) a computer is made, it takes several months to get delivery after the order is sent to the computer manufacturer. This means that the systems analysis must be based on what the company business and requirements will be at some time in the future. Since it can be expected that the installation of the computer will add impetus to the company's growth, it is generally accepted that a better plan is to base the systems analysis on business anticipated in the future (at least five years).

Costs obviously enter into the choice of computer. The computer business is highly competitive so that initial costs are proportional to value. A parallel-operated computer has more parts than a series-operated one and is thus more expensive. It is also faster. More dollars buy more speed. Likewise, more dollars buy more storage capacity. The necessity for speed and capacity must be weighted against cost.

Software is also a consideration. Are there programs available for the computer to do the specific tasks required in the business? Computer manufacturers maintain a library of object programs as well as compilers and assemblers. Thus, it is not necessary to write a new program if the job has been done before. Another consideration is the peripheral equipment that will be required, such as keypunches and other card-processing machines.

The answers to the above questions generally cannot be given by one man. The business executive in a company which has no computer usually has very little knowledge of the uses and advantages of a computer. On the other hand, the business data processing systems analyst may have an excellent feel for computer capabilities but little knowledge of that specific business. Therefore, the choice of a computer should be decided by a group rather than an individual. Frequently, it is better to bring in a team of management consultants who specialize in this type of systems analysis.

12–3   ERRONEOUS FEAR OF THE COMPUTER

When a new computer has been decided upon, there is frequently opposition from both labor and middle management. The workers fear that the computer will eliminate many jobs and put them out of work. The middle managers also fear that since the computer can make management decisions more reliably, they, too, may find their jobs eliminated. In point of fact, both are wrong. For the manager, the computer is just a better tool. If he learns to use it, he can perform his managerial functions with more confidence and more accurately than before. It is true that one manager with a computer can do what required more managers before, but the computer usually causes such an improvement in business that more people are needed rather than less. The same is true of labor.

A typical case is that of Eastman Kodak's color processing laboratory in Palo Alto, California. The company has an incentive plan whereby each employee's daily earnings are increased by a factor computed on the basis of how many and what kinds of tasks he works on during the day. This figure is calculated daily. Before the installation of a computer, six book-keepers were required just to calculate the incentive pay factor of the employees in the color processing laboratory. When an IBM 1440 was installed, this task was done by one operator in less than an hour each day. In addition to its other functions, the computer is now used for billing customers and making out paychecks. It is also used to keep track of film being processed and to determine the order of processing so that a maximum number of orders can be completed in a minimum amount of time. The result was increased business, requiring more personnel almost immediately. Where they needed six bookkeepers before for incentive pay calculations, none were required now, since the job could be done effi-ciently by one of the other clerks. But the six bookkeepers were simply retrained for other jobs, which were created by the computer. No one lost his job! In fact, more people were hired.

12–4 REAL TIME AND BATCH PROCESSING

One of the biggest advantages of a computer to management, but one of the most difficult to evaluate, is the concept of *real time*. Before the introduction of the computer, the manager based his decisions on reports of how the company had operated in the past. With a computer the manager gets up-to-the-minute facts whenever and as often as he needs them. Even with a computer, it is not always necessary to process data in real time, and this requirement should be considered when a computer is ordered. To process in real time means to get an output as fast as an input enters the computer. Thus, in the airline reservation system, for example, the information that there is a vacancy on a plane comes back almost immediately, when it is requested. This is real-time input and out-put. In a department store, sales slips are not processed immediately as they are written, but are entered on cards to be processed later. This is *batch processing*. Here processing does not occur as the event occurred, but data are collected in batches to be processed later.

12–5 TIME SHARING

When a company does not have enough clerical work to justify a com-puter, but management recognizes that some problems and decisions could be best left to a computer, the answer may be *time sharing*. It is possible to have many input-output units connected to one computer, so that information which is entered in a particular unit is processed, and the output comes out of the same unit. Since the cables connecting the input-output units to the computer carry only electrical impulses, there is no restriction on their length. In practice, a company buys one or more computers and then rents or sells input-output equipment to other companies that wish part-time computer service. The input-output unit is installed at the user company and connected by telephone line to the computer, which is centrally located. All the user companies share the computer. Since the computer works on only one problem at a time, this is called time sharing. However, since the computer solves problems in seconds or fractions of seconds, the user is always getting an answer almost immediately. There are many companies that supply this service and charge only for actual computer time used.

12–6   THE FUTURE OF THE COMPUTER

In the future, it is not inconceivable that computer service will be just another utility like gas or electricity. Every business, large or small, will be able to "tie in" to a computer by telephone and will be charged according to use. It is even possible that every home will have this service. Imagine, if you will, a housewife entering her marketing list on the input and receiving immediately the total that it will cost her in each of several markets whose prices are stored in the memory of the computer. She could then choose to shop in the market which will give her the lowest total.

There is no limit to future developments. Computers which respond to voice input or which have voice output will be developed. Try to imagine a conversation with a computer! Computers which read the printed page are already feasible. There will be input and output units which cannot now be imagined. Today's fantastic ideas become tomorrow's realities.

BIBLIOGRAPHY

BAUMES, C. G., *Administration of Electronic Data Processing, Business Policy Study, No. 98.* New York: National Industrial Conference Board, 1961. This report covers the planning, feasibility study, and systems study of 124 surveyed companies. Also covered are organizing the data-processing operation, selecting personnel and defining jobs, and improving employee cooperation.

MALCOLM, D. G. and ALAN F. ROWE, *Management Control System.* New York: John Wiley and Sons, 1960. This is the proceedings of a symposium. The topics covered are concepts of management control, research in systems design, new approaches to future possibilities in management control, and information systems.

QUESTIONS

12–1

How can the installation of a computer system increase a firm's productivity?

12–2

What is meant by EDP?

12–3

Give an example of how a computer could use linear programming to help management make decisions in the construction industry.

12–4

Describe the type of work done by a business data-processing analyst.

12–5

Why is there often resistance to the introduction of a data-processing system into an organization?

12–6

When might an organization want to install a real-time computer system?

12–7

What is the advantage of time sharing in a computer system?

12–8

If a group of cards (or other files) is saved for processing later, what is that group called in business data processing?

Answers to Odd-Numbered Questions

CHAPTER 1

1-1

The term "data processing" implies the collection and manipulation (processing) of data. It is not an end in itself. Data processing is a means to the end of using the data for some useful purpose.

1-3

1. To increase productivity.
2. To increase the speed of processing data.
3. To be able to process data more cheaply.
4. To better control the various business operations.
5. To process data more accurately.
6. To prepare management reports faster and therefore aid decision making.
7. To handle scientific and engineering problems.

Note: The list could be expanded to include: increase in "status" and reduction of monotony of certain repetitive jobs.

1-5

Businessmen in particular and the public in general failed to envision the tremendous potential of computers. Computers were thought to be so fast that a few of them could do all of the business data processing required in the country. It was many years before computers were widely used.

1-7

In punched card data processing, data are processed and reports are prepared by means of machines that can "read" the holes punched into cards. The data are represented by the holes punched into the cards.

Electronic data processing (EDP) involves the processing of data on electronic (not just electric) computers. Punched card data processing equipment may be used as input or output to the electronic computer, but the computer itself is the heart of the system.

1–9

False. The small businessman has several alternatives. There are many models on the market that are specifically designed for the small business and are cheap enough to be practical. Also, several businesses may get together and "pool" their resources to buy or lease a computer system. Another alternative involves the leasing of time (measured in seconds of actual use) on a centrally located computer.

CHAPTER 2

2–1

The governmental requirements of reporting and record keeping have increased. In order to have some sort of equitable basis for collecting taxes, the various levels of governments (national, state, county, and municipal) have set up standardized accounting and reporting procedures. These procedures often necessitate a huge volume of record keeping.

2–3

The buying and maintaining of an inventory of goods and materials is one of the most costly aspects of operating many businesses. Profits in a business are often measured in terms of the return on invested capital, and the cost of the inventory is included in the total of invested capital.

Data-processing equipment can be used very effectively to control the levels of inventory and to keep the average cost of the inventory to a minimum. This is accomplished by updating inventory records more frequently (often daily or even as the transaction actually takes place). By knowing the inventory levels more accurately, management can make better decisions on when to reorder and, in most cases, can reduce the average levels of inventory. Many companies have programmed computers to figure out when items should be reordered and even to actually print the purchase orders without any human involvement. The net result is that the total level of inventory is lowered, thus lowering the total capital investment and increasing the profit expressed as a percentage of invested capital.

2–5

Disbursing is the process of paying out money for any reason. Disbursing includes paying your own employees their salaries as well as paying for all of the goods and services your firm contracted to buy.

2–7

1. Recording.
2. Classifying (or coding).
3. Sorting.
4. Calculating.
5. Summarizing.
6. Communicating.

2–9

The list of various possibilities is rather long; however, some of the more commonly used *sorts* are:

1. To sort all the slips by department number and then sort by salesman number (to later summarize the amount sold by department and salesman).
2. To sort by department number and then by date. The goal here is to help management make decisions about the number of salesmen to have "on the floor" for the various days of the week.
3. To sort by branch number and then by department number. The goal here is to make performance comparisons between, say, the perfume department of the various branch stores.
4. To sort by department and then by dollar sales amount. The purpose here is to discover which departments have the largest average dollar amount per sale. Perhaps some departments should be eliminated because of excessive personnel requirements as compared to profit per sale and total sales.

Note: These are only some of the many types of sorts. The reader should explore other possibilities.

2–11

Part of the concept of communication includes written reports of data. Business data-processing equipment is designed to create these reports accurately and quickly and thus aid in better communication.

CHAPTER 3

3–1

He not only developed a system of faster and more accurate multiplication, but his ideas led to a wide variety of improvements in systems of manipulating data.

3–3

The materials and production techniques were so primitive that the machines were difficult to make and their performance (consistency and accuracy) left a great deal to be desired.

3–5

The ENIAC computer, built by the University of Pennsylvania in 1945.

3–7

Herman Hollerith worked for the United States Census Bureau and decided that the 1880 census took too long to process, i.e., it took too long to classify and summarize the data obtained from the census. He developed the first practical punched card data-processing system. He used this system in the 1890 census to record, classify, and tabulate census data. The 1890 census was completed in about one-half the time it took to process the 1880 census. Hollerith formed his own company to develop the machines. Through a series of mergers and name changes, the company became known as the International Business Machines Corporation, or IBM for short.

3–9

1. The additional cost of leasing the computer and then programming it to do a particular job may actually increase the overall or net cost of doing the job.
2. Since business data-processing equipment is often very expensive, management must shoulder the extra burden of controlling the activities of the computer to ensure the most efficient use of the system. Scheduling of computer activities is not only more difficult than scheduling manual procedures, but it is also far more important because of the high cost of the equipment.

CHAPTER 4

4–1

Yes. Business operations are generally concerned with the production of either goods or services. In the case of services, "production" and "delivery" usually take place at the same time.

4–3

Communicating.

4–5

1. Payroll amounts might be classified according to personnel working on the day shift versus those working on the night shift.
2. The company probably does cleaning for various types of firms. Jim's Janitorial Service would probably want to classify income and expenses according to type of business involved, to determine which types represent the most profitable clients.
3. Inventory items would probably be classified into the various types of products used in the business. This classification could lead to more effective inventory control.

Note: The students can probably think of many more ways in which the data might be classified.

4–7

Electromechanical equipment is run by electricity but involves the physical movement of a mechanical lever or relay to manipulate data. Punched card data-processing equipment offers an example of electromechanical equipment. Electronic data-processing equipment is again operated by electricity, but does not require any physical movement of levers or relays to manipulate data. The processing of data is done electronically, not with an electrically driven mechanical device.

4–9

To collate means to "merge together." In the business data-processing sense of the word it implies merging two files of records (which could be punched cards).

CHAPTER 5

5–1

The International Business Machines Corporation, commonly called the IBM Corporation.

5–3

"THINK" (often deliberately misspelled "THIMK").

5–5

Each punched card is an individual record of a single transaction. The implication is that the size of each punched card and the format of data on each record (card) are standard. Therefore, unit record processing is a method of standardizing the recording of a single transaction on each punched card.

5–7

One column or a group of several columns containing like information or data of a certain class is called a field.

5–9

Different corner cut, color, stripes, printing on the face, handwriting on the card, square corners versus rounded corners, and perforations differentiate one punched card from another.

5–11

It is one way of explaining how the cards are to be fed into the machine. Other ways are: 9-edge first, face down; 9-edge first, face up; 12-edge first, face up.

5–13

1. K = 11-zone punch.
2. F = 12-zone punch.
3. W = 0-zone punch.
4. L = 11-zone punch.
5. Z = 0-zone punch.

CHAPTER 6

6–1

A source document is the original piece of paper which contains the original data to be processed. It may be a handwritten record, typed, printed, or any combination of these. Examples of source documents are:

1. A sales slip made out by the salesclerk.
2. A record of a long-distance call made by the telephone operator.
3. A record of a gasoline purchase made out by the filling-station attendant.
4. A time card filled out by an employee.
5. A record of your meter reading of electricity consumption, made out by an employee of the utility company.
6. A list or record, made out by your receiving clerk, of what was received in your business.

7. The record filled out by you or your counselor, showing what classes you are programmed to take.

6–3

Alphameric (or alphameric field).

6–5

This statement is only partially correct, since a notch is also made when the machine detects an error in the punched card. The position of the notch is what is important. If the notch is in the right-hand edge of the card, then the complete card was correct. If, however, an error was detected, a notch is made directly above the column in error.

6–7

It would take at least 100 minutes with one IBM 557 Interpreter. Since the 557 prints only 60 characters per line, it would take two passes of the complete deck through the machine. The machine operates at 100 cards per minute. It would take 50 minutes for each pass, or a total of 100 minutes. *Note:* Actually, it would take even longer because card handling also takes some time. Therefore, to be technically correct, the answer would be something over 100 minutes.

6–9

Yes, it is not only possible but is done very frequently. Suppose that you were remaking your master file of inventory cards on January 5th of a given year. You could duplicate (or reproduce) the old deck into the new deck *and at the same time* gang-punch the date on which this operation took place from the first card into the second, and from the second into the third, and so on through the complete deck of cards.

6–11

To be able to vary the processing of data. On the IBM 88 Collator, for example, you might want to sequence-check card columns 1–9 of a certain file of cards, but on another file of cards you might want to sequence check card columns 5–13, and on still another file of cards you might not want to sequence check at all, you might want to merge with card selection. All of these processing changes are possible through the use of the control panel.

CHAPTER 7

7–1

As the IBM 407 Accounting Machine is printing the bills for each customer, the IBM 519 can be connected to it to summary punch a card for each customer, showing the account number and the amount of the billing. These cards can be used the following month as the accounts-receivable cards. They will be compared (matched with card selection) on the IBM 88 Collator to see which customers paid their balances in full and which still owe a balance. The point is that two separate and distinct operations can take place simultaneously— namely, billing and creating the accounts receivable file.

7–3

1. If the master deck is lost, destroyed, or damaged, the duplicate deck can be used as the master deck.
2. Several steps in the billing process can take place at the same time, thus speeding up the job.
3. Jobs other than the billing can be done as the billing is taking place. For example, inventory control, accounts payable, accounts receivable, and salesmen's commissions can be processed.

Note: The reader will probably think of many more examples of additional uses of the duplicate deck. The three answers given above merely represent the common uses of duplicate decks.

7–5

Now that the reader has a clearer concept of what data processing is all about, he will be able to discuss a wide variety of applications of data-processing equipment. Each suggestion should be evaluated on its own merits.

7–7

Not necessarily. There is a wide variety of data-processing equipment available on the market today, and some of the machines are specifically designed to do a certain job. For that one job, a particular machine might be the best approach, while for another job a different machine would be better. The point is that there seldom is a specific "right way" of satisfying the data-processing needs of any organization. The final choice is a compromise between the various jobs that need to be done and the best combination of machines to do those jobs. A systems analyst is the specialist who is concerned with this type of problem (among others).

7–9

In the past, most companies billed all their customers on the first of each month. Consequently, they had a tremendous volume of work starting on or about the 25th and going through the 5th or 6th of the next month and very little work to do for the rest of the month. It became obvious that this was a very inefficient and expensive way of doing the billing. Now, most organizations split their total volume of customers up into 6, 10, 15, or 20 groups and go through the billing process many times per month. The net effect is that the work load on both the machines and the people is evened out, the operation is more efficient, and the cost is reduced. This becomes especially important when you consider the large cost involved in leasing or purchasing data-processing equipment.

CHAPTER 8

8–1

1. The computer has a large storage or memory unit which can internally store numbers, letters, or special characters for later use.
2. The computer also stores the *program*, which tells the computer how and in what sequence a job is to be performed.

8–3

The control unit of a computer makes sure that the instructions or commands are carried out in the proper sequence. It also ensures that messages sent on the same wires do not collide. The programmer does not have anything to do with the control unit but he should recognize what it is doing.

8–5

It is considerably faster to retrieve data from the magnetic core unit. The retrieval of data from the magnetic tape (or drum or disk) involves the physical movement of the part in question (tape, drum, or disk). In a magnetic core, however, data are retrieved electronically and the process does not involve any physical movement of component parts.

8–7

1. The computer finds the instruction in core storage and transfers the instruction to the instruction register.
2. The computer decodes the instruction to decide *what* it is supposed to do and *where* it is supposed to get the data to do the job.
3. The computer gets the proper data.
4. The computer manipulates the data in the manner specified in the instruction.
5. The result of the manipulation is stored in memory.
6. The computer goes on to the next instruction.

8–9

1. Punched cards.
2. Magnetic disks.
3. Magnetic tapes.
4. Magnetic drums.
5. Punched-paper tapes.
6. Printers.
7. Cathode ray tubes.
8. Console typewriters.

CHAPTER 9

9–1

It results in a faster and more accurate method of manipulating numbers.

9–3

Most business computers use a special adaptation of the binary system of numbers called the binary-coded decimal (BCD) system.

9–5

Since four bits are needed for each digit, it would take three sets of four bits each:

$$0101 \quad 1000 \quad 0011$$
$$(5) \quad \ (8) \quad \ (3)$$

9–7

When a computer stops on an error condition, lights on the console indicate either *why* the computer stopped or the *location* of the command in core storage where the computer stopped. These "lights" are not in our decimal system, but they are in the particular code that the specific computer uses. Hence it is necessary for the operator or programmer to understand the code.

9–9

The parity check has already been explained above. However, it may happen that you have an odd number of bits representing a number, and yet there is an error. For example, if you had 1110 in the core storage of a computer using the binary-coded decimal system this would be an error, since only the numbers zero through nine are represented by any one set of four bits. You would not get a parity error because the number of bits in an ON state adds up to an odd number (three). However, you do have a validity error, since there is no such combination of bits in an ON state in the binary-coded decimal system.

9–11

No, it would take too long and is too cumbersome. Programmers use a special programming language that is later converted to what is known as *machine language*. This conversion process is done by the computer itself, not by the programmer.

CHAPTER 10

10–1

Programming involves writing a series of instructions (also called commands) to tell the computer (1) what the input data are like, (2) what to do with the input data, (3) in what order or sequence to manipulate the input data, (4) how to arrange the output data, and (5) how to output the data.

10–3

The address of an instruction merely refers to the internal core storage address where the instruction (in coded form) is stored. What is actually "stored" at that address may be an instruction (in coded form) or some other data. It is important to realize the difference between an address and what is "stored" at that address.

10–5

It stands for FORmula TRANslation. It is a computer language and is often used as a programming language in the scientific, engineering, and mathematical fields.

10–7

The program written in any computer language (like COBOL, FORTRAN, or AUTOCODER) is called a source program. It is usually punched into cards, one card for each instruction. A special program written by the manufacturer of the computer converts the source program to an object program. The object program is in machine language that the computer can understand and process. The special program written by the manufacturer to convert the source program to an object program is called a processor.

10–9

A system flow chart shows the overall flow of paperwork and operations that are necessary to perform a series of operations or one specific operation including the input and output. A program flow chart involves writing down in boxes of different shapes the flow of operations that must be performed by the computer to accomplish the task. It also shows the sequence in which the computer is to perform the manipulation of data.

CHAPTER 11

11–1

Because it can be used on almost all computers, whereas other computer languages were written for a specific manufacturer's computer. Therefore, if a company happened to have two different brands of computers, it might be more efficient in the long run to write all programs in COBOL, which would be applicable to both types of computers.

11–3

Names give you a convenient and easy way of referring to specific data that must be used in writing your program. For example, you might use the name "CARDDATE" to refer to the date field in the input from punched cards.

11–5

A file may represent a card file, disk file, printer file, or magnetic tape file of like data, whereas a record refers to a specific unit of data *within* the file. Hence, you might have a card file of name and address cards which contains *one card* for a specific customer. This individual card is called a record.

11–7

This division into parts offers a convenient and logical approach for describing to the computer what the name of the program is, the specific computer configuration to be used, the files and records to be processed, and the sequence of instructions to be followed.

11–9

No. If he did, the computer would assume that it meant a vocabulary word, not a *name*. Hence the program would not work properly.

CHAPTER 12

12–1

A computer can manipulate data much faster and more accurately than a human being can. A computer can increase productivity either by doing a given amount of work with *fewer people*—or by doing *much more work* with the same number of people. Either way, more work per individual is completed per unit of time, and productivity is increased.

12–3

Assume that a construction company is going to build a large apartment building. Not only are there many different tasks to be done, but certain jobs must be done before others. However, it is also true that in some cases more than one kind of task may be done by different people at the *same* time. (For example, the painters could be painting the outside of the building at the same time that the plumbers are installing the fixtures inside the building.) The computer could be programmed to figure out the fastest and most economical sequence of jobs and also which workers are to be assigned to which jobs to get the building completed on schedule and yet at the lowest cost. This would involve millions of calculations, so many in fact, that most construction companies would not attempt to figure manually all of the possible combinations. The computer, however, is ideally suited to make these millions of calculations and decide which is the best approach.

12–5

Some people believe that they will lose their jobs because of the computer. Others are afraid that the computer may indicate that their performance is not satisfactory. A third group may feel that they will have to relearn their jobs to fit in with the new system of doing things.

12–7

Many businesses are not large enough and do not have enough money or trained personnel to operate their own computer system, or their volume of data processing may not be large enough to warrant the cost of owning a computer system. In such cases, it may be to their advantage to share the cost of a computer system with other businesses. Each firm may have a separate input and/or output unit at its own place of business. These units—cheap in comparison to the cost of the computer itself—can be hooked up to a central computer via telephone company transmission lines. Each firm is charged for whatever time it uses on the central computer. This time-sharing plan permits each participant to enjoy all the advantages of computer ownership without burdening the firm with the cost involved in owning the system.

Index

Access, 79
  comb-type, 87
  random, 87
  sequential, 87
Accounting machine, 34, 59
Accumulating, 60
Accumulator, 76
Add-to-storage, 86
Adder, 76, 80
  full, 82
  half, 82
Address, 80, 101
Algorithm, 96
Alphameric (alphanumeric), 50
Analog computer, 25
Analysis, system, 133
Analytical engine, 23
Arithmetic logic, 80
Arithmetic unit, 76
Assembler, 102
Assembly program, 102

Babbage, Charles, 23
Batch processing, 135
Billing, 14, 30, 36, 68
Binary coded decimal (BCD), 93
Binary system, 91
Biquinary code, 93
Bistable, 90
Bit, 75, 78
Block, 126
Bookkeeping, 32
Buffer, 84
Business data, 13
  processing, 5

Business machine, 23
Business operations, nine, 14, 68

Calculating, 19, 31, 67
Calculating punch, 62
Card controller (UNIVAC 1001), 61
Card-reader, 56
  Friden ACR, 56
  IBM 557, 56
Cash register, 33
Central processor, 77
Channel, 83
Check, parity, 96
  validity, 97
Check digit, 97
Check register, 35
Classifying, 19, 31, 67
COBOL, 101, 111
COBOL words, 112
Code, 44, 93
  binary, 93
  biquinary, 93
  eight channel, 94
  excess-3, 93
  five channel, 94
  Hollerith, 41, 94
  seven channel, 94
  six channel, 94
  USS-6, 94
  weighted, 93
Coding (classifying), 19
Collating, 32, 57
Collator, 57
Collecting, 14, 30, 68
Comb-type access, 87

Communicating, 19, 30, 67
Compiler, 103
Computer, analog, 25
  choice of, 133
  digital, 25
  object, 119
  parts of, 75
  source, 119
Computer language, 98, 101
Computer simulation, 26
Computer system, 86
Computer word, 79
Computers, EDVAC, 25
  ENIAC, 24
  IBM, 1440, 86
  IBM, 1620, 25
  Mark I, 24
  SEAC, 25
  UNIVAC, 3, 25, 103
Configuration section, 117
Console, 77
  IBM 1447, 86
Constant section, 126
Control circuits, 60
Control panel, 61
Control unit, 76, 82
Core, 78
Corner cut, 45
Critical path analysis, 5

Data Division, 117
Data processing, 3
  EDP, 5
  machine, 4, 32
  manual, 4, 28
  punched card, 41
  system, 6, 86
Debugging, 129
Decimal system, 91
Decision making, 5
Deck of cards, 45
Decoder, 83
Delivery, 14, 30, 68
Digital computer, 25
Disbursing, 14, 30, 68, 69
Disk file, 79
Disk pack (IBM 1316), 87
Disk storage drive (IBM 1311), 87

Divisions of COBOL program, 117
Document, source, 48
Document orginating machine, 58
Drum, magnetic, 79

EDP, 5
EDVAC, 25
Eight-channel code, 94
Electronic data processing (EDP), 5
End-around-carry, 80, 92
ENIAC, 24
Environment Division, 117
Error check, 96
Error notch, 54
Excess-3 code, 93

Field, 44, 52
File description, 126
File section, 126
File storage, 80
Files, 64
Five-channel code, 94
Flexowriter, 56
Flip-flop, 90
Flow chart, 17, 104
  organization, 17
  program, 104
  system, 106
Forms, 30
FORTRAN, 101
Friden, ACR, 56
  6018 Disk file, 79
  2201 Flexowriter, 56

Gang punching, 58
Group printing, 60

Half-adder, 82
Hardware, 103
Hollerith, Herman, 23, 41
Hollerith code, 23, 41
Hopper, 48

IBM card (see Punched card), 41
IBM machines, 24 keypunch, 49, 64
  26 printing punch, 54, 64
  56 verifier, 54, 64
  83 sorter, 55, 64

88 collator, 57
407 accounting machine, 59, 65
519 document originating machine, 58, 65
557 interpreter, 56
604 calculating punch, 62
Identification Division, 117
Input unit, 77, 83
Input-output section, 117
Input-output unit (I-O), 77
Instruction register, 83
International Business Machine Corp., 41
Interpreter, 56
Inventory, 14, 30, 68, 113, 132
Iteration, 5

Jacquard, Joseph, 23
Jim's Janitorial Service, 28
Journal, 35

Keypunch (see Punch), 49

Label records, 127
Language, assembly, 102
  AUTOCODER, 102
  COBOL, 101
  computer, 98, 101
  FORTRAN, 101
  machine, 100
  MAP, 102
Leibnitz, Gottfried, 23
Linear programming, 5, 135
Listing, 60
Logic capability, 76

Machine data processing, 4, 32
Machine language, 100, 101
Magnetic core memory, 78
Magnetic disk file, 79
Magnetic drum, 79
Magnetic ink character recognition, 84
Magnetic tape, 77
Manual data processing, 4, 28
MAP, 102
Mark I computer, 24
Matching, 58

Memory, 75
Merging, 57
MICR, 84
Model, computer, 26
Morland, Samuel, 23
Multipurpose machine, 61, 69

Names, COBOL, 113
Napier, John, 22
Napier's bones, 22
National Cash Register (NCR), 35
  Model 33, 35
Nine business operations, 14, 68
Nines-complement, 80
Notch, error, 54
  OK, 54
Numerical punch, 44, 94

Object computer, 119
Object program, 102
Octal system, 91
Off-line printer, 85
OK notch, 54
On-line printer, 85
Ones-complement, 92
Operations research, 132
Optical reader, 84
Output unit, 77, 85

Paper tape, 83
Parallel operation, 82
Parity check, 96
Pascal, Blaise, 23
Payroll, 35
Peg board, 33
Peripheral equipment, 86
Posting, 32
Posting board, 33
Printer, IBM 1443, 86
Printing, 85
Printing punch, 54
Procedure Division, 117
Processing, batch, 135
  real time, 135
Processor (program), 102
Processor, central, 77
  IBM 1441, 86
Production, 14, 30, 69

Program, 34,, 75, 100
  COBOL, 113
  object, 102
  preparing, 103
  source, 102
  writing, 111, 118, 119
Program card, 52
Program code, 52
Program flow chart, 104
Programming, 98, 100
Punch (keypunch), IBM 24, 49
  IBM 26, 54
Punch, numerical, 44
  printing, 54
  reproducing, 58
  zone, 44
Punched card, 41, 42
Punched card data processing, 41
Purchasing, 14, 30, 69

Queuing theory, 133

Random access, 87
Read-punch machine, 83
  IBM 1442, 86
Read/write head, 78
Real time, 135
Receiving, 14, 69
Record, 9, 42, 115
  unit, 42
Recording, 19, 30, 67
Register, 83
Reproducing punch, 58
Reserved words, 112

Scanner, 84
SEAC, 25
Selecting, 58
Selective printing, 60
Selling, 14, 30, 68
Sequence checking, 58
Sequential access, 87
Serial operation, 82
Seven-channel code, 94
Sight checking, 59
Simulation, 26

Six-channel code, 94
Software, 103
Sorter, 55
Sorting, 19, 67
Source computer, 119
Source document, 48
Source program, 102
Sperry Rand Corp., 41
Stacker, 48
Storage, 75, 77
Summarizing, 19, 32, 67
Summary cards, 66
Summary punching, 59
Synthesis, system, 133
System, data processing, 6
  total, 6
System analysis, 133
System flow chart, 106
System synthesis, 133

Tab card (see Punched card), 41
Tabulating, 60
Tabulators, 34
Tape-storage unit, 77
Time sharing, 135
Typewriter, 77

Unit record, 42
UNIVAC, 41
UNIVAC 1 computer, 3, 25
UNIVAC 1050 computer, 103
UNIVAC 1001 card controller, 61
USS-6 code, 94

Validity check, 97
Verifier, 54

Weighted code, 93
Word, 79, 100
Words, COBOL, 112
  computer, 79, 100
Work area, 117
Work storage section, 126
Work storage, 80

Zone punch, 44, 94